A Renewed Outlook
On Early Education

The Wrong ABCs of Preschool

Setting Your Expectations
Right For Your Child

SHRUTI NAGAR DAVE

INDIA · SINGAPORE · MALAYSIA

Notion Press Media Pvt Ltd

No. 50, Chettiyar Agaram Main Road,
Vanagaram, Chennai, Tamil Nadu – 600 095

First Published by Notion Press 2021

ISBN 978-1-63904-710-9

CONTENTS

From the United States

Deergha

***5.0 out of 5 stars* One of the best books for parents, Highly recommended**

Reviewed in the United States on August 18, 2021

Verified Purchase

Best book on early childhood education. It's an important phase in children's lives and the author of this book has mentioned everything with real-life examples and experiences that we need to know when we have younger kids at home. Must have book for parents. Highly recommended.

Reema Arora

***5.0 out of 5 stars* New era of Awakening must read**

Reviewed in India on 1 September 2022

Being an Educationer for a longer time. I feel pride in reading this book. This book is a new era awakening. We really need to acknowledge even pre school is important for Child Development and how much it is and it can help in building a better human being for the future.

Amazon Customer

***5.0 out of 5 stars* Must read for both parents and teachers!**

Reviewed in India on 31 August 2022

Being a teacher myself, I recommend this book to all parents and teachers who are confused on which parenting style to follow. Though the parenting style can't be one for all, the guidance in the book will help you to figure out yours!

Amazon Customer

***5.0 out of 5 stars* One word «EXCELLENT»**

Reviewed in India on 31 August 2022

I started reading an excellent book written by Shruti Nagar Dave ... wondering how we (parents) miss the child's perspective of the world to them ... though we all want the best for the child... this book will open a new point of view of parenting for the both (child and parents)... I request all the parents out there to go and buy this book or gift for your friends...

ABOUT THE BOOK

The challenge of what to expect in preschool years and from preschool persist because of multiple available theories, options and unawareness of research. I have been working with teachers, parents, children and schools at unique levels and what I see as a closed-door is the lack of collaboration amongst them. Each one has its own approach, expectations and struggles. Working in school and preschool, I discovered that it is vital to have a voice of the entangled view and open the platform for all stakeholders to discover together (i) what is the purpose of a preschool, (ii) what do children need in foundational years, (iii) what is the role of adults in foundational years, and (iv) what can we expect from preschool. With my hands-on experience, this book seeks to present the voice of a child, teachers, parents and an education enthusiast. We generally think that preschool is all about teaching children the required content, prepare them for formal schools, make them get comfortable with reading and writing, help them get social, learn and stay engaged. That's alright; however, these are not the only expected outcomes or the key outcomes for preschool years. This book has chapters defined based on eight common expectations of adults from children in preschool years. Each chapter has real-life examples and experiences that would make us all discover what the root of the expectation is and what we can do to alter the same to make it relevant to the child. I have added reflections after each chapter for the readers to reflect upon their thoughts and bring the action to life. This book is for parents, schools, teachers and other people associated with the early years of education to explore the idea of the purpose of learning in early years.

ABOUT THE AUTHOR

Shruti Nagar Dave started young as a visionary founder of a Trust, The Should Be Education, India. She has served for 10+ years in the Education Industry in diverse roles such as philanthropist, curriculum designer, academic research, trainer and has been enterprising in her vision. Educating parents and teachers on what children want from the child's perspective is how she began to speak for children by working with NGOs, schools, educational institutions and publishing strong messages through her blog. Her work has been recognized by national and international organizations, and she has been a recipient of various awards, such as, Karamveer Chakra Bronze as well as Silver (2015, 2016) Rex iCongo UN, Quality Mark Women Awards 2016, and Global Minded (Denver, Co, U.S.A) 2019.She has also served as an Ambassador at HundrEd. She is passionate about adding an open-minded approach to learning experiences. She has developed and designed curriculum for different pedagogies and approaches like Inquiry Approach, Understanding by Design (UBD) (thematic) for primary years and early years under IB, C.B.S.E., State boards, Progressive schools and alternate schools parameters in India.

She has a background in management, education and design. She is only and first receiptient of HighScope® Trainer Certification in India with endorsement of HighScope Preschool Educational Approach. She advocates the HighScope approach in the early years of education and has worked around its implementation, curriculum design, teacher training, parenting webinars and lesson planning at Footprints, India. The learning never stops hence she continued working on her research and doing multiple courses through credible organizations on clinical psychology for young people. She has a certification in HighScope Preschool. Besides, she has been consistently working on herself to grow deeper as a spiritual seeker. She published her first book in February, 2021 *The Soul's Mind*, which has set the tone for her as an author and her future projects.

NOTE TO READERS

I have put my heart into this book. It is a combination of what I have learned throughout my career in the education world and from people who have reached out to me with their concerns around providing a better environment to their children. I have worked with children from early to 12 years of age and I see my reflection in them, and hence this book is a personification of the inner child within me who wants to come out and express the emotions and experience that children have while growing up. This is my first step towards giving a platform to adults in understanding the foundational years of children from an open mind. I am looking forward to continuing this journey and share more such life experiences with my readers in my upcoming projects. Therefore, I would urge you to be accepting of this ideology and feel free to share your experience by working around the practices, given in each chapter. The Reflection pages are for you to put down all your thoughts and help yourself discover a new outlook for the role and purpose of adults in the foundational years of children.

INTRODUCTION

I began to design activities when I was a child. My sister and I and a few of my friends spent time designing games, plans for weekends, scripting movies, learning new skills, and more in our non-school hours. I began running my own drawing class when I was only 10 years old and called our neighborhood children and asked that I would teach them drawing for Rs.3. When I was collecting coins, my mother laughed and asked me to give back the money and told me that I must not ask for money. I felt that I was giving a service in exchange for money, so why should I give it for free. I can still recall those days and laugh about them. I knew somewhere that I was a bit off track from the race. My life has been full of miracles, if I really look into it, and that's when after 29 years I realized that I have been blessed and the supreme power is always keeping an eye on me to protect me. It's only when you realize it, you can feel it. I never understood schooling and their educational approach till I graduated. I waited to get out of it so that I could do what I liked. As a child, I was the most misunderstood child as far as marks were concerned. My mind was always in a conflicting state as I struggled to figure out why should I write what is written in books rather I would write what I understood from those books in my own words. But the expectations in primary school involved writing what I was taught word to word. I did not really get the 'factory model of education'. I was an active child and ended up participating in various cultural events to escape from the race. I thought the board wasn't right for me so I changed to C.B.S.E. after my 10th grade. I did pretty well in specific subjects and enjoyed studying, however, I forgot that in the end the knowledge of a student is always assessed based on his/her memory skills. Yet I stood out and I was selected as a school captain by teachers and the school principal. I felt I was on top of the world and was reassured in the knowledge that there was room for being different. Yet disappointed from the whole ranking and teaching method, I promised myself that one day I would open my own school where children would learn based on their choices and explore life skills. I called the project 'Guruschool'. If you are reading this, trust me if it is destined to, this project will take shape soon. However, as I said, being unconventional, I do get questioned by conventional minds. I began my research and came up with ways I could bring the Guruschool project to life.

While I was in college, I joined the vision of Ms. Janki Vasant, Founder of Samvedana Trust in Ahmedabad. I was blessed to have such hands-on experience in the education industry from the ground level and explored the space by continuing in counseling children, designing curriculum, training teachers and creating unique projects to engage children at school. Eventually, as I said I was a passionate learner and a creative, unresting worm moved across my brain, I ended up doing other degrees to figure out what I really wanted to do. Another elevation was when I joined Redbricks Education Foundation under the vision of Mrs. Renita Handa, Founder of the school. She taught and trained me to create planners based on Understanding by Design (UBD), and I am grateful to Mrs. Renita Handa for introducing me to the possibility of having a program for self-enrichment for young children. It was a coincidence to be working on this as it was one of my dreams to have such content taught to children in their early years. I cannot thank enough both the organizations for trusting my talent and passion over anything else.

I got married and moved to Gurgaon and that's where my next level of discovery began. Well, I did what I did and ended up meeting a lot of education leaders, parents and teachers for different purposes. In 2016, I joined Footprints Preschool as they were looking to set up their curriculum and delivery. I guess, it was all destined and there I began my mastery in an approach called HighScope and got my certification from HighScope Education and Research Foundation, Michigan, USA. I studied HighScope and God was too kind and blessed me with this opportunity to contribute to children, schools and teachers with the active learning approach which was one of my core beliefs. I got my certification in HighScope preschool curriculum and to date, I haven't stopped researching and creating programs and initiatives that work best for children. I am amazed and thankful to schools, teachers and education enthusiasts who have trusted my path and have constantly encouraged me and have reached out to me for their concerns and allowed me to contribute to their children's development.

In 2020, I became intense with practicing mindful studies and meditation. I developed inspiring connections with people through various online courses. One such course was by BOD Consulting, and that was a milestone for me to discovering what I am doing and if I am in the world, what is it that is at the core of my purpose. Every experience I have had in life is magical. It happened as it was meant to be and I acknowledge it as that. My sister, Miti Nagar helped me make a breakthrough in this space. I have been since then, implementing mindful practices in my daily routine and that has moved me to a different power altogether. I am grateful to her for working with me on this. That's when I began my work on this book. I had powerful self-discoveries that ended up having a root cause in my childhood. Why do I have such fears? Why am I behaving the way I am? Why do I feel stressed? Through these seven odd years my husband, Mihir Dave, has been a pillar of strength to me in achieving so much and living an extra ordinary life with a rich spiritual environment at home as well as high companionship. For all my extreme, diverse and risky projects I have never heard a no or a doubt or lacked support. If this book is happening, it is because of his encouragement. I could not have asked more in life. To be married in a family that is serving Hari Guru, is one of the greatest blessings of my life. Guru Kripa is the source of my breath and it has provided me with a skill to see opportunity in anything that knocks on my door. I believe I am a daughter of the universe; Hari Guru. And I could give a lot of people credit here however the true power is God and his grace on me. People who help you or care for you are the medium for God to deliver his messages. He is within you, and that's all. Life is about discovering that you are a soul and all you are doing on earth is discovering that reality that under the influence of the materialistic world 'maya', we have simply forgotten. So to all the people who were in fact medium of God's plan – my friends, my teachers, my coaches, colleagues, family, clients – and people who have inspired me to keep my faith to transform education world, I thank you all! Hope this book makes you proud of the times we worked together. My mother, Naina Nagar and father, Deepak Nagar, for being great support. God has blessed me in a lot of ways and, sometimes I get numb when I count the things I am grateful for.

I took my notes, videos, research, books and blog one day and reviewed them all, and while doing that, only one voice came out unsettled and that was the wrong ABCs of preschool. And that's how this book came to life.

I want to acknowledge that I am nobody, but a learner. I am nobody but once I was a child, I am nobody but I did learn about the struggle of some children, I am nobody but I could empathize with the challenges teachers have to face, I am nobody but I do get the anxiety of parents, I am nobody but I understand why we need more schools. I am nobody but a learner forever. I continue to research, work and bring out more for the world as a responsible educationist, and I always strive to be a courageous one to stand up for the missing key and shout out to all stakeholders of the education world to bridge the gap by making the learning foundation for children strong in their early years of life.

It is just this, when they say "the sooner, the better" or "catch them young"!

Happy reading and reflecting!

– Shruti Nagar Dave

ACKNOWLEDGMENT

Practicing what you preach is one thing and writing a book on it is another. It took my heart and soul to write this book and each word that is written came from my own experiences as a part of the education community. You could find brilliant books around that will provide so much knowledge for sure. However, I wrote this book to express and record my voice and what I believe in. Besides, I want to share with people recommendations for high-quality early years education and various studies by institutions that I believe to be effective. I want to thank Mrs. Janki Vasant for trusting my creativity and approach towards children and education, Mrs. Renita Handa for providing access to progressive and child-centric curriculum creation, Mr. Raj Singhal for all the opportunities to contribute to the education world.

I thank each and everyone I have worked with and exchanged learning and inspiration that has made me who I am today. My sister, Miti Nagar who has an exceptional mind for making learning innovative, creative and logical. I thank my entire family, specially my in-laws who have always stood by me no matter what.

This book is inspired by and dedicated to Teachers. Finally, I am thankful to my spiritual *guru* and Radha-Krishna for their grace on me. I have not learnt about spirituality or the discovery of who I am by reading books; my mind is not powerful enough to comprehend the existence of the divine. It is because of my spiritual Guru's *kripa* (Grace) and God's love that I feel a connection with the almighty and feel more at peace with myself.

CHAPTER – 1

IT IS NOT ABOUT LETTERS AND NUMBERS

"I wish we were more worried if our children missed out on compassion, empathy, courage and creativity than missing out on remembering a few letters and numbers."

– Shruti Nagar Dave

“It has been six months my child is in a preschool and yet he cannot recognize all the letters, also my neighbor’s child who is three years old can rote count till 100,” a parent at a meeting shared. I did not know whether it was a question or sorrow of a disaster a preschool made by not forcing children to learn letters by heart and also rote count till hundred. I mean they could have just focused on the goal and would have ignored the exploration and discoveries the child was making each day at a preschool, right?

I did not want to add sarcasm just at the beginning, but it just came out naturally so would let it be. Upon reading the quote given at the begging of the chapter, some of you must be thinking, *what a cheesy and cliched thought to begin a book with*. And here I’d like to pop that bubble as everything that is not practiced or not easy to abide by, we call it cheesy. Say, you hear someone tell you ‘one must always be polite’, what would you say? “What a thought!” Or “Why don’t you implement it first in your life?” Well, I used to be that one who leaned on the latter side but then I realized that the opportunity to learn was killed the moment one invalidates what is being said by comparing and judging from our past experiences.

I am a normal human being who lives and operates from how a child feels about the environment and perceives the world —not as an expert or a parent but just as a child. Hence, I gathered the courage to write this book and become a voice for normalizing the learning process. Learning is a natural process; we adults have made it so structured and significant for our children to fit in the world and we conveniently tag children with a problem that we fail to resolve for them and there are people making money based on those fears.

How many of us get worried if a child missed saying 4 after number 3 and jumps to number 5? What is your reaction if your child mistakes b for d? How patient are you in nurturing a child with a deeper and experiential learning process? How many of you say, "I told you this a hundred times and you still do not remember it!" Well, I am sure when you say 100, you mean twice or thrice. Adults exaggerate their efforts by wearing a blanket of self-pity. I have sacrificed my fun, watching TV, going out with friends just for the child and many of us say this to others in front of our children. And there goes the environment that invalidates the poor being who is so perfect and in a natural pace but is being attacked on confidence. By now, I may have offended many who are parents and who may start to have infinite thought bubbles, but I am not writing this book to speak what is obvious but to express what is happening in the brain of that little child while we sing our fear, worries, anxieties, self-pity and effects of social pressure.

If you've reached this paragraph, I want to thank you for trusting me so far and walking with me to explore and discover more about the 'First Wrong'. There are different methods and ways how children learn letters and numbers, now here I am talking about literacy. So, why do we want our children to learn letters and numbers? From the list given below check the item that speaks for you:

1. So that the child can learn to read faster;
2. So that the child can learn to write;
3. So that the child can get admission in a formal school by clearing the admission test (well, I will highlight this in Chapter 2);

4. So that I can call my child a smart kid; and
5. So that my child can match with the world.

*'the world' in the last point we speak about is an imaginary world we create where we see the future of children from a limited perspective. This includes sending your child to a school where they can become future-ready and opt for careers like engineering and medical in the future. We only expect to prepare children to go to top universities like IIMs and IITs. And that puts a lot of pressure on children and they feel disoriented in terms of their natural abilities.

Well, this description of the 'world' I call a 'Monster' from a child's perspective. The whole book is a voice of 0-6-year-olds as there is still some hope to nurture the brain so that the peace we talk about is attained, you know why? Because the adult brain is full of doubts, questions, mistrust and prejudices, so the word 'peace' would conflict with betrayal. Whereas young brains have no prejudices unless parents share their perspectives, so if these children are exposed to a positive environment full of hope, exploration, trust, and a sense of community, they are going to be the adults who will have peace that will synonym to oneness, trust and unity.

If you checked on any of the points above, it is a sign of you being one with me right now. So, let us together explore the purpose of letters and numbers as a part of preschool.

First of all, learning letters is part of language development and I would break it into four unique purposes:

1. Language;
2. Literacy;
3. Communication; and
4. Expression.

Language

Language is a system of communication that contains a set of sounds and written symbols.

Literacy

Literacy is the ability to identify, understand, interpret, create, communicate and compute, using printed and written materials associated with varying contexts.

Communication

Communication is the act of sharing or exchanging information, opinions, ideas or feelings.

Expression

Expression is the act of expressing or setting forth what you feel or think in words.

Well, there are millions of books and theories available in the market to learn about how language development takes place in the early years. I recommend you visit highscope.org for extensive research and studies on early years education. But let's look at it from the non-academic side. How do we learn a language?

How did you learn the language you speak at home? Who taught you that? Did you go to school to speak the first word? Or it just came out? How? You were not technically taught letter sounds? The best way to know what the child wants is to reflect on what did you want as a child, and, I guess, that would take a lot of work. To be able to recall, one must first recognize the happenings and share the same. People like me are so much into marking the learning sources that we can picture how we learned the words we use in our daily life. I still remember the time how my brain learned the word 'umbrella'. I always found this word difficult to understand because I just could not connect with letter 'U'; I found it unnecessary as a child as I wasn't sure about vowels and consonants. Later, in one of my drawings of the umbrella, I related the stick of the umbrella as 'U' and that is how I bonded with that vowel.

Some of us might find this funny or insignificant but that is the whole point. You eat up all the theories or meet branded experts or celebrate founders from the education business, but there will still be that one unidentified way that one in a million child would be waiting to be discovered. I mean it is a lot of work, isn't it?

A preschool is a place where children explore the language through the environment. Now here is a catch – the environment around children defines their learning and how they see the world. Many parents ask me about how I will teach reading and writing to their children. To this, my simple answer is, "they will learn what they listen". This implies that the primary objective of schools and parents should be to provide a language-rich environment. Language rich environment is where the objects, areas and walls are labeled, have visuals with text or caption and adults speak to children in proper sentences and use vocabulary that children will use in their day-to-day life.

You must have noticed, some of us keep away bigger words from children thinking they yet aren't aware of letters, so they will not understand or remember the bigger words. For instance, adults talk to children as they are kids however they need to speak to children as they speak to any adult. I have heard parents use the word '*mummmumm*' for 'food', while they offer children food. And after some years, the same parent would complain that the child still uses the word '*mummmumm*'. Well, do you think it is a problem with the child? Is he or she not saying what was taught to them in the foundation years? Let's look at this one, when a parent complains about the child not eating without YouTube, who at first introduced the practice?

What to expect in the area of language development in preschool years? This could be the next question that we could discuss to get an understanding of Developmentally Appropriate Practice (DAP). We can consider the following scopes in the preschool years:

1. **Enjoying Language:** The development here is about the experience of listening to words, dialogues and conversations through children's interaction with adults, books, songs and peers.

2. **Exploring and Playing with Nonsense Words:** One of the things that will help children get fluent in speaking and reading the language is to first understand the role of vocabulary in preschool years. When we talk about vocabulary, we are actually talking about four related vocabularies. In terms of the length of vocabulary, the order from largest to smallest is as follows:

- √ Listening vocabulary (words we can hear and understand)
- √ Reading vocabulary (words we can understand when we read)
- √ Speaking vocabulary (words we use when we talk)
- √ Writing vocabulary (words we use when we write)

For younger children who are still learning to read, speaking vocabulary is generally larger than their reading vocabulary. But for older readers who are past the "learning to read" stage and who have entered the "reading to learn" stage, this is the typical order.

The conversational method is an effective way to help build your child's vocabulary. It is an indirect method that is so simple that you can start using it right after you read this chapter.

In a nutshell, the conversational method is simply talking with your child and expanding the scope for unfamiliar vocabulary.

- **Step 1:** When a new word comes up in a conversation or in a book, provide a simple, age-appropriate definition for the same.
- **Step 2:** Provide one or two examples that make sense to your child.
- **Step 3:** Encourage your child to think of his own example, or of the opposite of the new word.
- **Step 4:** Use the new word in your conversation over the next few days.

When showing them how plants grow while you are gardening, using the word 'photosynthesis' is necessary even if you are talking to a 12-month-old child because the intention here is to tell what the process is called, and this is a part of conversational style vocabulary. In other words, parents and teachers must keep in mind not to use any alternate 'non-sense' words, such as *mummmum*, but rather use appropriate vocabulary. The question here is—why do parents use short words or made up words as vocabulary in the first place? Because they think that the child won't understand, which is a misconception. Later, the same parents complain that their child is two years old and he or she doesn't use proper words. These common errors come from adults' perceptions and understanding of learning levels. My recommendation is to read research and study it or follow the school's standard milestones that help us keep track and check on the current learning levels of children.

These words are expected to be part of listening vocabulary and not reading or writing vocabulary. If you want your child to develop richer vocabulary then expose them to meaningful vocabulary. Do not count the letters in the words rather teach words while having a conversation with them or contextually. While you are cooking, when your toddler is around, do not start babbling to yourself, but use phrases and conversation such as: "I am going to cook vegetables for you today, a nutritious food; it will have the right amount of nutrients, right? Yes, you are smiling, I notice that" (describe how your child is responding)."I have tomatoes, spinach... we will let it steam for 20minutes, should we? Ya? Hmm. Let me see what ingredients I will need to make it." Now, even if the child is a newborn, using exact words like ingredients, steam, nutrients, etc., will help your child get a language-rich environment.

The reason children lack vocabulary is that they are restricted and adults around them do not use the labels and words with an understanding that children won't get it. Focus on providing them a language- and vocabulary-rich environment, as per the developmental stage they will store words and later when they reach milestone they will relate the words and will not struggle in spelling or writing them as they are already aware of the context where the word is used.

When we look around media and information randomly it might get us confused and impact our child's natural learning desire, as our expectations would come from inappropriate resources and standards that might not be relevant to our children. Hence, it is vital to refer to research and data from credible institutions.

Reflection:

1. What is the one thing that you found interesting to read in the first chapter?

2. What would you like to change about your usual view about preschool years?

3. What is the one thing you would like to share with your friends and family?

4. If you had to change one thing from your preschool years, what would that be?

CHAPTER – 2

IT IS NOT A PREPARATORY CENTER FOR FORMAL SCHOOL

"If your curriculum doesn't encourage the thinking process in children or challenge them, it is a source of an unthinking future".

– Shruti Nagar Dave

I will share an episode from my formal school life before I talk more about the role of preschool in this space.

[The Last Rank]

"Good morning class, we have an inter-school essay competition on July 16, 2000," announced Mrs. Patel. She was my class teacher, strict looking but always ready to help. I loved to see her in the classroom. She carried two-three books and a red jell pen every day to class. I felt like I was her favorite student because she dropped her eye at me when she explained anything in the class. Anyway, this announcement made my day, as I was bored of regular classroom sessions. Now, this is what I was waiting for. I always looked forward to competitions as I knew I would shine out. I desperately waited for Mrs. Patel to ask for us to raise our hands if we wanted to participate. Mrs. Patel said, "So, we have selected all the top 10 rankers to go appear for the auditions". Bad luck! Had it been the last 10, I would have made it. But wait, what did essay writing have to do with the memory test results of the class that happen every month in school? And that's how I was tagged and labeled forever. Additionally, based on the marks I was moved from Section A to Section B in the same school year. Hilarious it was that we children knew on what basis were the class sections made.

I wasn't ashamed of not writing exactly what was given in textbooks. I never understood why does one remember and memorize things from the book and test memory. If it was about a history chapter, why weren't we asked to write what did we think about the Battle of Panipat, and what could have been the possible ways to resolve it? As a 10-year-old, I felt like I could go beyond it, but all the 35 years old never got it. I wonder what it would be like if children are not ranked but asked for the choices and skills they wish to develop or explore. I don't know, well it is always the rank system that defines what's good and what's bad. Look at the world today, people go by the ratings, and filter options based on ranks or scores or reviews, and people ignore the stuff below the top five. How do we know that the reviews or ratings and ranks are genuine? I know one guy who cooks delicious food, and many people would visit him daily. Poor guy, he has no clue about the Google Reviews or social media to get more people. I asked him once, "Why you don't buy a smartphone and actually put an Instagram post with pictures of your food, and you will get more people."That young, skinny happy guy looked at me with his confused eyes as if I was talking to him in gibberish. And he said to me something which sounded like, "I don't know what you mean by more." I shut up and learned something beautiful. It is certainly your choice to be on whichever side you want since 'more' is an undefined term that makes you feel that you always have less. If you know what is more, you will be in a state of dissatisfaction. However, if you have no "MORE" in your world, you are happy, satisfied and focused on your work. *Stay Hungry* is a great slogan for health but not for your life.

A10-year-old me hated this fact as it wasn't the first time that the selection was based on ranks in the class as it had become an established criterion. I started feeling low, awkward, and inefficient as all those top 10 rankers were my friends, but suddenly Mrs. Patel clearly said in an unclear statement that I was not a fit in that group. Well, that was the biggest crime in 'childhood law' that Mrs. Patel made. I am sure if she is alive, she is still not aware of it. Which school would have taught us that? Which educational framework has a rubric that says you have what you must have, and you can have anything you want but you will have what you should have, and life has it for you? To my readers, if you understood the previous line, consider you are beyond "more".

(the bell rings) Recess time. I saw Patil bhau going near the bell from the second door of my classroom. Well, no wonder that became my favorite seat as I could see outside the jail and get out first. BLA BLABLA... is what I heard now as it was Mrs. Deshpande lecture, and I did not really care even if she caught me being inattentive because it was 10 seconds to recess. And I was all set to run.

Well, were you able to relate to the kind of school experience I have had? I mean sure if you are a like-minded person, you would certainly understand what I am saying. Now, reflect on where you are today in life. How happy are you? Does being a top ranker in your academic life have anything to do with your happiness?

Preschool years are amazing years where children experience a transition from home to school. For example, at home, they have their own personal space and set of toys, but when they start going to school, they learn to share a common space with other kids. I would like to share what exactly preschool does to a child when he or she is a part of it. It makes a child explore the world outside them; it helps them to explore and appreciate the art and sciences of the environment; it gives them an opportunity to contrast their own knowledge with help of their direct interactions with materials and people (referring to HighScope approach); it allows a child to see that there are differences and it teaches them how to respect those differences; it helps them to make choices and decisions starting from who they want to play with to which toy or material they would like to explore? What are the things they do not like? They get a chance to appreciate the diversity in the classroom and so in the world, and thus a foundation is laid for how they will be receiving and perceiving the world in front of them.

Now then, I hear a lot of such conversations from adults where their anxiety of future is about when will my child learn numbers till 100? Can you please teach my child some general awareness, it is be part of the test paper for taking admission in a formal school? Let's stop here and do some thinking. The world highlights merit-labeling and so do formal schools, and this is the reason board system still exists. If that is the kind of future people are made to believe, then it is natural to look at preschool as a preparatory center.

With such beautiful aspects of life skills that children get to explore, why is there a need to destruct their natural desire to learn by coming from a place of survival? If you look at it from where I see it, it is more about adult's unclarity and mistrust with the future that leads them to direct, drive, force and sketch the kind of life a child must have. I want to say out loud, "*Children are not born to be inclined towards things they like, they do so because it is the only thing fed to them in their environment, and that is wrongly perceived by adults as the child's interest; it is what you feed them, it is what they are surrounded with, it is what they are told or shown, it is what they consume from the environment designed by adults.*"

What is then preschool's role in preparing children for formal school? I am sure you must have this question. Well, definitely something that this chapter will serve. One day I was at school where I worked and met parents who came to look for preschool admissions. I was inspired to have an opportunity to be able to share the unique learning process that the school served and talk more about the approach. When I began my sharing, I was stopped right then and some parents asked me, *"that is all fine but do you prepare children for formal school admissions?"* I was in my beginning stage of my career hence I kept my words and experience with me and answered, "Yes, we do". Later I was curious and could not stop asking them a question which was, 'may I know what is that supposed to mean? What do you expect when you say preparing for formal school?' And they responded, "*Yes well, the entrance test that the child will take for English, maths and general awareness.*" I reconfirmed, " are we here talking about a three-year-old child?" And that made me stunned for a long time as to what we are doing here. We are trying to limit the tender age of exploration within a box and schools are acting as apparatus for manufacturing scholars and high scorers. I realized that it is not about what market demands or parents expect, the entire system is in a trap where the only stakeholder that is dealing with adverse effect is the 'child'.

Preschools give a unique space to children to prepare for future or formal school by providing them with their own space to explore. These school serve as a great opportunity for children to dwell in their own curiosities and inquiries, experience the sense of belongingness, understand other's space and pace, learn to share and live as a community, understand and respect diversity and culture. How many of you are willing to be open to uncage children with this purpose of preschool? How many of us are no longer worried about various entrance tests our children will be taking to get an admission to top schools or universities, but rather have bigger view in mind — encouraging children to prepare for their entry into the world of exploration?

A young mind visited preschool one day with his parents. The moment he entered the preschool he wanted to run to the play area and play. He was tagged as a Down syndrome child. Well, I was keen and curious to have him in the school. I asked the mother, "So what is it that we can do?" Listening to her words made me light the fire to make difference right away. She said, "The preschool he is going to currently is not willing to have him continue and they have given up. They said he cannot make it to normal school hence we should take him to a special kind of place." For a couple of minutes, I was literally in flame and thought of giving it back to the one who said this to this child. I held myself and requested the mother if I could just observe the child for a while. She was fine with it. While I headed to the play area, she called me out and said, "Do whatever but just let him come to school." I controlled myself from promising anything and just nodded. The child seemed so conformable in the school and did not shy away from the teacher and curiously explored different materials. Looking at the scene, I realized that the child was away from all the judgments and conversations that could limit him, he was full of expression. I had made my call that this child deserved to express anyway.

Every child deserves an education — education to live life, create life and design life. Not the life that puts them in a box to act and behave as adults of today do. None of us know what the future holds, however, our fears, insecurity, the arrogance of the known and ignorance of the unknown stop us from exploring the space of freedom, choice and play.

I called the mother and said that I have got her back and I got the child. She was so happy about the fact that her child would be going a school. Apparently, it was not as good as it looked to me because a couple of days later, few parents complained about the discomfort they felt at the thought of the boy sharing space with their children as they thought that he was not normal. Their words hit me hard. But since that is not the subject of the book, I would like to inform the readers that it is an accomplishment for the preschool as it succeeded in nurturing that child in such a way that he is now receiving his formal education from a credible school. He also ended up giving some dance auditions and making everyone proud. Do you feel this magic or it is just me? The magic power of trust, faith and a learning environment. I have so many instances and experiences that made me connect with children to an extent that their interest and scope have now become my priority while I design curriculum or provide research and training.

So, if we are talking about preparing children for formal schools in a way that they express themselves as they want, they explore spaces as they want and they have a sense of competence over rush to just win and complete the task, then yes preschools do prepare young minds for formal schools.

A few years ago, we were taught to develop good handwriting and writing speed. How much of that is relevant today? In our school days, we spent a great deal of our time learning and memorizing answers for our school tests, how much of that is relevant today? Instead of fixating on what we think is right for children — which is often a result of our own failures, fears and judgments that adversely affect the freedom and choice of children today — our job is to promote exploration and participation in life. No matter what the situation is, it is all to be explored. It is important to ensure that our past experiences do not define the present of our children, and we should always strive to set an example for our children by living in the NOW.

I am aware of schools that take entrance exams to assess the competence of children as young as three years old in order to decide whether to give admission to the child or not. I have spoken to parents who opened up about their application being rejected as the child could not pass the English test. I do understand that the role of assessment here to learn more about the child's learning and pace. When a child transitions from preschool to formal school, the school has no history of the child's learning style, so it may want to know about the same as one of the ways to collect information about the child's learning style, pace and level. However, just rejecting the application of a three-year-old child because he or she could not score marks, makes zero sense. In my opinion, it is an outrageous act.

"This is one of the important factors that has made young parents insecure about the child getting into formal school hence their demands from early years are formal, instructive and destructive for children and our future." -Shruti Nagar Dave

Whenever I doubt my own experience or thoughts, I ask myself what worst could happen? What would be the impact on me, my family and the world if I take this action? The answer I hear from myself helps me take the call. Likewise, in this scenario, who is more impacted? Children. If a school that is comparing and fitting children in a box is rejecting your application based on a memory test, would you really want your child to be associated with it?

We generally find ourselves hanging out with people who are like-minded or have similar opinions and views as us. Why? Because confronting people with different views can seem like an intimidating task. Put yourself in a group of people where their views contradict with yours. You would not like to be around them anymore, why? Not because they are wrong or bad people but because you find it difficult to embrace new perspectives, which causes discomfort. However, the general idea says that real growth and enhancement happen when you are out of your comfort zone; and this is the same approach we apply while nurturing children.

The irony is, we all want our children to succeed, however, the path that we imagine comes from our own drawn comfort. Before we expect anything from children, it is important to be in a position where we are able to teach them by our own behavior and actions, as children learn by observing the environment and people around them.

In terms of former school readiness. Uh, in early years, children need the following domain to be worked upon: (i) physical and motor development, (ii) social and emotional development, (iii) learning language, and (iv) cognitive development. These are the key skills that we need children to develop. These goals, as per research on early years of education, were accompanied by an analysis of the role that early intervention and demonstration programs, or pre-schools, primarily those developed and tested with toddlers, play in promoting the 'focus-readiness' dimensions.

Children learn a lot by going to a pre-school because they become exposed to numbers, letter shapes, concepts, stories, rhymes, active participation in play, an intentional play designed by teachers and so on. But more importantly, they develop social and emotional skills and learn how to get along with other children, share and contribute. Research shows that children who attend high-quality preschools develop better pre-reading skills, richer vocabularies, and stronger basic math skills than those who do not. So why not focus on and invest more in pre-school education.

Here are some reasons why a preschool is good for your child and how it helps children to prepare for school readiness:

- Firstly, pre-schools provide a foundation for learning both socially and academically. In the early years, children have a natural desire to learn, explore and see things. They are very, very observant. They learn by exploring different spaces and experiences they gather from their interactions with teachers, peers and objects. Children explore tasks that make them independent in their daily life.
- Second, a preschool is an opportunity for children to be in a structured setting. As it says, that daily routine is so important in the early years of your child's development that it sets up children and channelizes their energy. It is an opportunity for children to be in a structured setting with teachers and a group of children where they learn to share and follow instructions. Participate actively, and you will know a lot of other things that they keep doing during their mealtimes, playtime, outdoor-indoor interactions, storytime and so on.
- Thirdly, preschool will prepare children for further schooling where things get more academic. So don't be afraid of the fact that since the focus of preschools is on skill development, it will be overwhelming for children as it consists of an important part of their curiosity and development. These will not cut their playtime. Every child deserves a high-quality

childhood education. In fact, these types of schools are based on learning through intentional play, or you can say active learning, to be precise.

I remember an incident when I had a parents-teacher meeting and the type of questions parents asked and the doubts they had. These included: "My child is too young for books and to be part of the learning environment. I just want my child to play now." Here's the thing. Parents feel that sending children to a preschool or typical preschool will take child's time away from play. However, we must first define the meaning of a high-quality preschool. High-quality preschools are those that focus on active learning i.e., their programs, their time and their settings. Their daily routine is all based on intentional play. They take care of choices of children, their interests, the development they need, and the contents that are supposed to be delivered in terms of concepts. It seems like they are just having fun or playing, as the teacher knows what sort of materials and toys and games that she needs to setup and what is the development that she's assuming that will take place; besides, she will be observing and taking anecdotes to help parents understand the development that has taken place and how they can support it at home. So it is a kind of teamwork that parents and teachers need to build.

In the next chapter, I'm going to talk about how parents can sometimes become indifferent to the child's development once admission to a preschool is done. Things like, "we are paying you", "teacher will know better", etc. can make them think that their job is over. Let us discover what exactly is the role of a parent and teacher as a team.

Reflection:

1) What would you say to those who judge children by their power to memorize numbers and words at a tender age?

2) What would you say to the schools that conduct entrance tests to assess the eligibility of a three-year-old child based on his or her score?

3) What was the one thing you were awestricken by in this chapter?

4) Whom would you like to share your learning from this chapter with?

CHAPTER – 3

IT IS NOT ONLY ABOUT TEACHERS

"Preschool years equals resourceful environment, freedom to learn at one's own pace and trusting the caregiver and research".

– Shruti Nagar Dave

"Are your teachers certified and trained?" she asked. "Yes, we do train our teachers in the approach we implement," I replied. "Ok, so what are your hiring criteria and what is the highest degree for eligibility?" she added. Meanwhile, I struggled to understand the significance of the question and come up with an appropriate answer. The question took me to a scene in the past where a young toddler of 10 months needed a diaper change in between the class; a two years old child threw the meal bowl of the other child; three years old children fighting for the same toy in the class; a four years old child being fed during the online class. Now, why these situations? Hmm, think about it. These are the common situations encountered in a class of toddlers and preschool children be it online or offline. Whilst this is on, the caregiver or teacher, or educator is also focused and planning on teaching concepts by ensuring the engagement level of the child is intact. Which degree will teach anyone these skills? Which degree helps educators experience the uncertain and un-vocalized issues the child may deal with? And if at all those degrees exist, how many of us will continue to be a teacher after graduating with a specialization degree or certificate? Won't you start your own school or get work in administration with this level of expertise?

Well that, my readers, is the highest level of respect humans could get from children. They love teachers because teachers listen to them when they wish to be heard. How many of you remember your early years' teachers? Or the person who took care of you? It disheartens me when I hear comments for my preschool teaching community like "it's a nanny's job"; "the pay is as low as pocket money"; "there is no career growth or prosperity in this job".

Interestingly, these comments aren't just from the people who take the service but from the leaders who run schools. They are the pillars of the organization or school and that sets up a tone for others as how they treat each other. The tone you hear from parents or community for teachers is the tone set up by the organization, period. It has been more than 10 years now for me to have a great valuable bond with the teaching community. What I understood being a teacher is that if teachers are trusted by school heads, founders, co-teachers, parents and community for what they do, the impact of their care, teaching and nurturing is higher. I still remember when I was teaching Grade 2 in Redbricks Education Foundation. I was 21 years old then. The first and the foremost foundation set up by the principal and the founder of the school was that they trusted me for my creativity, passion and what I spoke in my interview. I do not remember to have spoken about my degree, but the conversation was at the peak with the degree of my passion for education. Now that was my foundation and the only thing that kept me on with confidence and commitment. Internally, I did know I was young and how my parents would react to me, however, I was told that they were giving me the most active classroom to teach and nurture along with the opportunity to design curriculum. And that was not all, the founder, I would call her my mentor, she gave me an amazing opportunity to design a self-enrichment program, which was all based on mindful studies with her. With this richer foundation of trust, I look at the teachers I have in my training and the organization I work with. I see them as my mentor saw me then, but what is it that they aren't receiving the power I am sending them time and again? The answer was since I was at the source of the organization, so no matter how much I talk, it will have a limited impact as my word is not the last word in their employment.

This makes schools or organizations critically responsible for teachers' mental health. Unfortunately, I haven't come across any school that acknowledges this part. Schools and organizations must understand that occupying teachers' weekends in the name of workshops or meetings is not taking care of them, appreciating them once a year does not help them either. What they need is respect, a day off and a strong foundation that introduces them as power.

Now, that looks simple however it is not easy for people who doubt their self-worth or are in an insecure space. Some people like to show authority by dominating and keeping them in superior positions because they know from the inside that they aren't an authority. There is fear that they will lose their position or attention. The people who are authentically authoritarian are the kind of leaders who listen, who are secure, and they know who they are. Those are the leaders we need in the education industry. Another irony is that schools preach progressiveness, but for their teachers and staff, they give precedence to the hours of work they do over the impact and quality they put up in the company's vision.

That was something!! Let me share what teachers do and experience. I am proud that this is a cumulation of at least 80-100 teachers I have interacted with and or read about. In preschools people say that the teachers who join aren't passionate or that's not their primary job, they do it may be because they are bored at home or not able to find a job elsewhere. On the other hand, for those who are highly qualified in society, like a Ph.D. or master of education or even certified in NTT or equal programs, how many of those are willing to teach? None. Here is the true essence of who should be a preschool teacher. A preschool teacher is a highly conscious, humble, and patient listener and a caregiver who understands the learning and emotional needs of the child along with their health and hygiene. She or he will take care of the developmentally appropriate levels for children by taking required training on the subject. He or she is committed to learn and continue to educate themselves by incorporating practices that are relevant to the generations (the needs of a 10-month-old is different than that of a two-year-old, hence the term 'generation' is used) they work with.

If this person is a teacher of your child, then this calls for a celebration as you have met the right person. I remember once I was talking to the mother of a 10-month-old child and I was showing some open-ended materials and their impact. She asked several questions, and when I said that she may be right however the research I was referring to could be trusted as it had its own credential, and maybe she could look and read more about it as she was interested to know more and it would help in working with the child at home. I was surprised with the response I got from the mother, she said, "Hey, do not say trust the research or teachers. I have a double degree and I have read about some programs in early years on Google". I simply smiled in pity that while she said all of that I could only hear 'insecurity', 'fear' and 'guilt' and 'arrogrance'. If Google could help you know everything, I guess 80% of the services or businesses would have been shut down long ago. We neglect the importance and value of experience or on-ground work after reading few articles on the internet.

What are we trying to achieve in these cases? Nothing. Who is getting impacted in the ego clashes between parents and schools? Children. What is at stake when we do it? The future of the world. Because the child is learning what he is watching, listening and is consuming from his or her environment.

It is time for us to unlearn and let go of the negative, unproductive and unhealthy conversations and doubts we have about preschool teachers. Instead of asking for their qualifications, ask about ways or strategies they will be using when your child is feeling uncomfortable in a new space. Understand strategies and partnership opportunities from them and work together to nurture children in their early years and provide them with a strong foundation. Spend time learning about the educational approach the school follows and figure out ways to set up a home environment in alignment with the approach so that your child feels connected and confident in the process.

Trust your child's teacher, research and experts' work. The care given by a mother and a teacher are different; set your expectations right. Your doubt and vibe will make your child uncomfortable with the teacher in the foundation years. Children will settle only if their parents are settled. It is not a wonderment that there has been a lack of trust in the entire system. Earlier the case was so different. I have seen this transition very closely from a school at the core of education to the business model at the core of expansion. The energy flows from the top, so if the people who run schools are intending to grow it as a business model with least interest and investment in the educational research or what children want, they aren't going to be at the source of the purpose of school. It is saddening to see this expression or vision getting diluted to an extent that it is now about who runs the school (credibility from A-listed graduate schools) over anything else. There is no one to blame though, it is a two-way process where what you are doing is getting the kind of response it deserves.

In preschool, all we hear is which brand it is? Who is the management? Is it trending? Which celebrity is promoting it? Do they have a history? And the list is endless. What if we were more focused on what does the research say? Where is this research coming from? What does the developmentally appropriate education look like? What does my child need and what is the learning style? The world would have been different. The top institute graduates are willing to create a business in education. Why? Think about it!

I have worked closely with teachers and I get more power from my own teaching experiences. I remember I was a Grade 2 teacher as well as curriculum developer years back and all I kept in my mind was to walk through the path to gain experience to be able to set up my own school. With each day passing by, I encountered challenges, stress and frustration a teacher goes through. I remember, I was in the classroom and I struggled to engage children in learning a concept as the children were out there in their own space of curiosity. I was under pressure to complete the course and deliver what I had planned . Eventually, I just gave up and went to my co-teachers in the staff room and cried. They all stated, being experienced teachers, that it is what is it, and it is ok. I worked hard to build trust amongst the children and became one with them, eventually, there was this time when I went out of my comfort to search, design and come up with ways that each child in my class was served with the best of the resources. The focus was to be understood as a teacher and understanding what children need. I realized that if I keep myself at the center of the class, I would end up making a mess and losing an opportunity to nurture the best in them because all I would care about is how good I am as a teacher. But my breakthrough as a teacher was when children were the center of the class and their needs were above mine. That is when the stress turned into a refueled passion for education. I wish teachers read this and they really listen to what it reads to them, that the power is within us – power to transform how education is perceived. If I talk about preschool teachers, I guess there is a lot of work we need to do as far as establishing the highest value of the service they provide. This job deserves the highest pay. It may sound like a cliché, however I am not worried as far as it is authentically expressed.

It won't be difficult to re-establish the state of value preschool teachers carry as we only need to listen to what they have to say, acknowledge their efforts in nurturing children and collaborate with them in preparing for the future.

Reflection:

1. How will you connect with teachers from now on?

2. What is an ideal preschool teacher for you from this moment?

3. Share an incident where the child became settled with teachers in just a few days? What according to you made this happen?

4. Mention five qualities of your child's school teacher that made you trust him/her?

5. Write a letter to a preschool teacher restoring his/her valuable position in the education industry.

Your letter here:

CHAPTER – 4

IT IS NOT JUST FOR PLAY

"Success has nothing to do with winning; it is the lifestyle of a person who seeks to learn at every step in life."

– Shruti Nagar Dave

I could never have learned to ride a bike if I was not free to play, I wouldn't have experienced what is to be a teacher if I hadn't role played as my class teacher; I would not know what happens in the kitchen if I did not play with my kitchen set. How many of you just had flashes of memories of your time playing and exploring. Play is an underrated term now. Some of us think that 'play' means free time to do whatever the child wants. In this chapter, I will help you view 'play' from a development perspective. At the end of this chapter, you will look at play as an important part of a child's development and also an important space for adults to remain creative and alive.

Let me share some definitions of play before I instrument it for educational purposes. Some common definitions are as follows:

"... engage in activity for enjoyment and recreation rather than a serious or practical purpose."

"Play is a range of intrinsically motivated activities done for recreational pleasure and enjoyment. "

"Play can be viewed as the natural vehicle by which young children learn, yet may be pushed aside in favor of work or more formal academic learning."

There have been people who preach education philosophies and prioritize the needs of children instead of just catering to the demands of adults by training children to be part of a rat race. It's funny, schools have their mission statements and tag lines such as, 'Preparing children for future'. Be it exact words or some other, they do mean to say that each school prepares children for their future.

Parents, on the other hand, work for children's future. And what is this future? Have you ever thought about it? Which future each one of us is considering? What is our basis to define the future? How do we know what is going to work in the future? How do we find out what jobs or opportunities should we prepare our children for? What are the kind of resources our children need? What skills are going to help them survive? Well, survival is all that all the species worry about, right? How many of us went off track and opened up our view to shift our focus from making children learn new skills to making them live in 'now'?

There is no definite answer to the above queries. If I put it differently, let's face it, we adults have been trained to live in a manner, we have our own patterns to work on, and those patterns and experiences come in between children and us. We are trained to be survivors and look at what is in for us. What do I get if I do this? We are always looking for getting something in return. We were not taught some of the key skills that would have given more weightage to the idea of 'living' rather than 'surviving'. I would like to share my view on this with you right now, say, reflecting on the patterns and discovering importance of adult's role in nurturing children.

Before we talk about what the future is preparing children for, or is it even an appropriate mark or vision, let us first reflect on what we have become. Get your pen and diary to write down what comes to your mind when you read the questions. Once you have the same, settle in a space, close your eyes and breathe about six times. Deep breath – inhale and exhale x6. Breathing is a magical and powerful way to calm our mind and get into the present.

- What was the important skill that you feel grateful to have learned in your early years?
- Reflect on your life and list down five happy moments. Just five.
- What do you regret not learning in your early years?
- Mention two important values of your family, something that most of the family members preach.
- What are you frightened of?
- What makes you give up?
- What are five important values you want your children to learn?
- What are the three things you remember from your early years' memories?
- Write two things that make you differ from how you behave at home and at work?
- Mention an incident from your life where you stopped expressing yourself, if any. It won't be in totality, however it may pertain to a disconnect with one person or more or a situation.
- Do you remember anything that adults, at home or school, in your life said to you thathas impacted you forever?
- What are the words when said to you trigger you the most?

Answering the above might take you a while. I appreciate each one of you for reflecting on it and getting in an uncomfortable space to get close to yourself. Just so you know, the context of this exercise is to make you wear children's shoes and open your minds to relate with them as your partner beings. If you look at children as an individual, you would definitely do good to them. Looking at them as children and by calling them 'kids', adults tend to refute their imagination and vague ideas. Of course, once in a while, say it might have been a conscious effort to hear what children say however I say 'mostly'.

So, what did you find? Did it refresh your memories and take you to your childhood? If any of the answers you could not fill in, I suggest you make take a fresh attempt the next day. It is always better that way. What is it like to be a child? Imagine the curious, confident and high-energy beings are showered with adults' fears, anxieties, worries and failures every day. Children feel that their progressive beliefs are being questioned when they hear statements like "don't do it", "you never let me work", "you are disturbing me, I am on important call", "this is so easy, how many times should I teach you", and so on. These were enough to damage the confidence of children and make them rebellious as all they want is to be heard.

The future is in now. Now is what we all are never taught to live in, and being content is never framed as a successful stage. We are trained to thrive and strive. But for what? The whole life, many of us kept striving for success, but, what is success? Is it about having more money, name and fame? Then why aren't those who have all these things not happy? Does this striving for 'more' ever stop? What is the end of success? Is there a place where this ends? A person walking along a street sees a guy on a bicycle and dreams of having a bicycle. When he gets the bicycle, he feels happy ridding it until he sees a man driving a car. Then he starts dreaming of owning a car. When he gets the car, he feels happy driving it until he sees a bigger car (I heard this analogy from my spiritual guru, Jagadguru Shri Kripaluji

Maharaj, in his lectures, and it has just stuck with me ever since. It helps me whenever I need to work on being still and appreciate what I have). The pattern goes on and on, without putting an end or attaining contentment with what we have. Our children are in this environment and they are watching and observing their surroundings. These children are going to grow and become the same adults as we are. And that, my friends, says more about what kind of future we are nurturing.

Children learn best when they participate actively in daily life experiences, so it becomes the topmost responsibility of adults to ensure that the surroundings are full of hope, wisdom and creativity.

I would like to share some cases with you about some ways we could disorient children with an environment that doesn't teach them the importance of self-love and thus, make them detached from the real world. Recently, you all must have seen that Instagram, being an app for 18+, has more feeds of children. So, the adults are fed with videos and posts videos of children. Funny though, children have no idea about what is happening. Sure, some argue that those are the memories and life timelines for those parents like infant's photoshoot, how they walk and talk videos and all. Many parents in fact make children speak on subjects that promote hatred, well it may be disturbing for children to grow in a world where they see bad things. What will they turn out to be? We must prepare them and share stories that give them more faith and hope, that will make them believe in good and upload the same goodness and compassion when they are dealing with others. I guess it all began with mom bloggers, which I believe was a good initiative though for mothers-to-be or mothers to get some ideas and support in terms of parenting and nurture a community that cares.

However, few manipulated this concept and turned it into a tool to get fame and presence by putting videos up for likes, views and followers. I mean, I spoke to many about this in my circle, and some said it is not what we should promote and some called it a mere act of entertaining oneself. Sure, but this entertainment is proving to be worrisome in terms of the child's mental health.

I do know there are billions in the world, and I am not sure to how many this book will reach, but it is encouraging to know and even if one like-minded person in a billion hears me out, this would give a push to the needs of children. We are the ones who built this unnatural fascination among kids for social media, such as, YouTube so that we could find some peace time while they are busy watching videos and other stuff on the internet. Once the same child gets addicted to social media, parents start to figure out ways to get them out of this vicious circle. Sad, but true. I am sure every problem has a solution and those who are willing to resolve do find it at their rescue.

So, a preschool that works on an active learning approach has its core in 'Intentional play'. Intentional play is a form of play where the learning goals are defined with help of materials, language and people as part of the environment. For example, playing with educational material may involve giving play dough to children to play with. Play dough is given to the child, and adults participate in their play as partners and say, "I was wondering if you would like to make some shapes and numbers using this play dough". This is intentional play, here the learning goal is exploring numbers or recapping shapes and numbers the child knows so far. If the adults, either in school or at home, use rich language, complete sentences, new words each day, the child consuming the same will have stronger vocabulary and language.

There are some intentional play ideas I am sharing with you as an early years curriculum specialist and HighScope advocate. Try one of these every day to encourage meaningful learning experience for children at home or at preschool.

1. Role play

Many of us have had great memories with role plays. Playing teacher, doctor, chef, businessman, vendor, vegetable seller and many other roles. What does it do? It helps children to learn about the concepts or importance of community by experiencing the role. They learn new words related to respective roles, dialogues and use language appropriate to the play. This helps them increase their vocabulary during the play as these it involves, concepts like history, diversity, community, empathy, and problem-solving, which is an essential component of the learning process. A child playing the role of a chef or a doctor implements all of his or her experience and how they perceive the role in their play. I remember I was in one of the centers where I worked and there I observed a child (three years old) wearing a white shirt and using a doctor set. He prepared a corner that looked like his clinic using a table, table cloth, sticky notes and markers. He made medicines by crumpling small pieces of paper. I role-played as a patient in the play and he prescribed me medicines, saying, "play two times a day and here is your medicine". I asked him, "it must taste bad, right?" He said, "No, it tastes like chocolate". And I observed the paper he wrote on, it was an exact imitation of a doctor's handwriting. He may not be fluent in writing letters but he scribbled as if it was a doctor's writing. If you are wondering how this matters and what children will learn, then here are the skills he learned: (i) pre-writing skills; (ii) new words based on the role he was playing, such as, 'medicine', 'taste', 'breathe', 'well', 'bed', 'patient'; (iii) problem-solving skills; (iv) imitating and pretending (creative arts); (v) learning to see things from a different perspective; and (vi) counting (he said 'two times').

Pre-schoolers are engaged in learning as they explore. They do not need separate study time. It is up to adults how and what they observe and later help children move to the next level of learning. So you can make the role-play learning-rich by offering children open-ended materials and working with them as partners by having them lead the play.

2. What is in the basket?

Children show interest in inquiring and exploring materials. They need a versatile and holistic approach to have an exploration that is developmentally appropriate and fulfills their natural learning desire. This activity promotes a learning experience that is focused on sensory play, exploring materials, vocabulary, classification, sorting, story building, learning about textures, patterns, colors, and shapes. Let us explore how to make and implement the basket activity. Find one, low-sided basket, and label your child's name on it. Capitalize the first letter of the name as children learn to read the print in the environment. Even if the child cannot read, labels are a must as part of the whole language approach to reading and writing; children would learn by seeing the tag and listening to the word from adults. For example, where is your name written? It is here, point out each letter, give letter sounds and read the full word or name. Now you will need indigenous materials of a wide range of different textures, weights, colors, shapes, smells and sizes that are designed to be explored by young children. The objective here is that the materials offer a wide sensory experience, hence, these are also be called sensory baskets.

What are the different concepts children can explore while engaging in this activity?

They will experience what is smooth, rough, pliable, rigid, soft, shiny, cold, heavy, light, round, and/or angular. They will explore different sounds that the objects or materials make like a bell, spoon and plate, glass and roller pin and hollow objects or dense objects. Other concepts they get to easily learn related to pre-mathematical skills are big and small, same and different, and heavy and light.

In order to have specific exploration based on concepts, you may also create different personalized baskets like fruit basket, vegetable basket, toy basket, wooden basket, sand or water tray and so on. Let me share an example of one of the activities that are part of pre-writing skills. By offering children a fruit basket, they learn names of fruits, what they taste or smell like , what they look like from the inside, and how they are different from the inside and outside. They will also explore peeling fruits, such as a banana, and this will help in developing their small muscles, which is a part of the pre-writing skills activity. Other popular activities for developing pre-writing skills involve sand tray, play dough, tearing-pasting, making newspaper balls by crumpling them.

The basket activity does not only make children explore the materials but it also helps them to see things from different views. For example, during a play, they get a chance to explore their creativity and imagination as they learn to manipulate objects and situations to use them according to the plot of the play and keep turning its context by adding materials and new information. As a part of safety measures, adult supervision is highly recommended. You must use materials of bigger size and rounded edges to avoid any hazards. Avoid using any material that could include toxins and chemicals e.g., wood should be unprocessed (not varnished or painted) and for metal items, look for those made from stainless steel. These are easily available in our kitchen. Avoid using items that contain small parts and/or small balls may invite chocking threat. You must schedule your time to check the items in the basket at regular intervals, sanitize them and then provide the same to children for use. To keep the child engaged, I recommend adding one new thing in the basket each time. For example, you can add a family photo sometimes, or a small mirror, washed socks and so on.

3. Save the toys

This activity is my favorite. I evolved this activity from one of the experiences I've had working with children using one of the HighScope resources. This activity is focused on science and problem-solving. You need to prepare for this activity a day ahead. Bring an ice tray and bring some of your child's toys (small-sized, for example, animals and cubes) now put those in the tray and fill with water and keep it in the freezer to freeze. The next day, tell your child that we have got a problem. Some of our toys are trapped in this tray and they won't come out. We got to save them. Ask the child to come up with solutions for this problem. You need to implement and try out each solution children give if it is feasible. And eventually use ways to unfreeze the toys. Mostly, adding lukewarm water will help solve the issue. Once the toys are free, say, "You solved a problem". The critical part here is to ask them to share what worked. How did we save the toys? Now, here the emphasis is on the learning process as the questions you ask them would help them retain the information in the long run.

4. Broken toys

We do experience that many children have broken toys still in their playing area. Sometimes, the parents are not aware of the broken toys and at other times, children would not let you discard them. In this case, what to do? We know that keeping broken toys can cause injuries so, here's what we can do. Using some 'best out of waste' ideas, make something with those broken toys. For instance, if the kitchen set is broken and it has items that are small in size, then use the broken pieces; and if they are uneven or big in size, break those items into smaller ones and fill them in an empty bottle or jar and seal the cap. You just created a sound box or a sound (sensory) shaker out of the broken pieces. It is valuable to create and do the process along with the child. You can say, "I noticed that your toys are broken and I don't want you to get hurt by letting you play with it. I wonder if I could help you create a new toy by using it. " This way you will have your old toys in form of a new toy. Would do like to make with me? Let us create it together." Set up a dedicated corner, bring all materials you need and now step by step work on it by describing the process and actions to children. This will give a sense of ownership to the child as he or she will experience the importance of being co-creator in the process. In case you find yourself struggling with gaining your child's attention, then all you need to do is make them part of the process and see how they take charge of it.

The idea here is to nurture the natural desire of children to learn. Even the broken toys can do so much if the context is set right. That is the baseline when we say, play with the context.

5. Young chef

In this activity, having children prepare their own meal by planning, discussing and choosing ingredients from the choices you give them, works like magic. It is simple, the moment you decide to take responsibility for it. So, when a mother serves food on a plate and ask children to eat, there are chances that they might decline, ask for something else, or may eat what is give to them. However, what gets missed is responsibly eating and being grateful for the food we get to eat. The approach that works, in this case, is modeling the behavior we expect from children. When children see how and what adults do with the food, they begin to imitate them. Say, if mom or dad uses mobile while eating, or watch TV while eating, do we really expect that the child is going to be eating food all by themselves without the screen? Then we criticize children for being stubborn as they wouldn't eat unless they are allowed to watch TV or YouTube. Now, this does not only impact how they consume food but also impacts their health and thoughts. By thoughts, I mean their energy levels. So, prepare some options with the help of children. These may involve decorating Monaco biscuit with cheese, tomato and coriander, or coconut balls, however, make sure the process doesn't include heating or baking. After their job is done, you can ask them to relax by saying, "Now, mummy will do the rest of the cooking as it is not safe for you to do it". Giving a proper and correct reason for why you said no to the child is very important in building the relationship. The way you communicate your ideas or reasons with them will impact how they relate with others or situations. So having them participate in meal planning, grocery shopping and cooking will work like magic as this is a critical life skill where you make your children learn to be independent at a very young age.

6. Swapping story characters

Bring in the classic stories that children love to listen to or any story that they'd like you to read to them during bedtime or any time of the day you have set up as a routine, and recall the entire story with your children. Now, ask them insightful questions where they will be required to do some thinking and employ their problem-solving skills using their past information to come up with some work that depicts their social and emotional development. For instance, the children pick, *Red Little Riding Hood*\. Now you must have read stories several times, and children may also have pieces of their imaginations and connections with the story's characters. You will now ask children to swap the characters, such as, imagine a wolf that's innocent and the girl is wearing a green hat and any other changes you can think of. Now, offer children ideas such as, "Hey what would happen if the little girl had an access to the phone, would she have called her granny to tell her about her trouble?"; "What if you were the wolf, what would you have done?". Well, there are many stories in which the endings usually involve either hitting or killing or making someone a villain. These are the stories that must be avoided at any cost because stories have a unique power to turn around the perception of children, which is based on hope, love and peace. This activity not only helps in language development but it also does helps adults in bringing up a mindful and skilled future of the world.

Pay attention to the source and words of the classic stories and rhymes before you make it your child's favorite. For example, you must have by now understood that rhymes and songs, such as ring around the roses, Humpty Dumpty, Jack and Jill, etc. are no longer relevant to the children as these involve miserable themes, such as a disease. Of course, you can Google this information and get an idea of which rhymes to really preach.

7. Gardening

Nature is a healer, and we all belong to it. You must have had planting activities with children and wondering what more this activity can do as I mention it as a part of this book. So here me out, this activity has a bigger purpose than it what it appears on the surface. The environment that is provided to the children in foundational years weaves their pathway to perceiving the world outside. Mostly, this is why family values are carried naturally by members of the family. The environment includes the language that children consume, colors, items and materials they see around, conversations they listen to day and night and kind of food they are served. The environment also includes the vibe and energy the children are surrounded with all the time. So if in a family the adults argue aggressively and fight in front of children, children sense the vibe and take the heat and eventually they also end up handling a conflict or problem as they have seen their adults do, with aggression. Likewise, if in a family the wisdom is humility, acceptance and spiritual the way the child will perceive life will be cooperative.

So all you need is to have only one plant, if you aren't fond of it, and nurture the plant by watering and taking care of it. Just as if it is a pet to them and children are responsibly taking care of the plant as a living being. What will this do? This will make children responsible beings. They will experience what is it to give life. What happens if I forget to water the plant even for a day? They will explore how old leaves dry out and fall off and then new leaves are born, which is an appropriate example of manifestation of life. Some people find it depressing to talk about life or death. However, I feel that we must prepare our children in a manner that they are future-ready to find a true purpose in life by getting involved in the present moment than worrying about the future. Imagine the kind of citizens you will gift to the world as parents or teachers.

8. Involving children in daily chores

I have met inspiring parents and teachers who are open to offering young children some real work, like washing toys, laundry, cleaning up the play area, sorting and arranging clothes as per events, categorizing toys in the basket based on desired attributes. These activities normalize the fact that we help ourselves with these daily tasks and live independently in daily life. Some adults feel awkward about allowing schools and teachers make children do such tasks. I remember one incidence which I would like to mention.

In July 2016, one of my colleagues, who was taking care of a class in a school, shared the following incident with me — "Today, a parent was furious and they might withdraw the child as a teacher was making a three-year-old tie their own shoe lace and making them wash the toys that they used. The parent mentioned said, 'We are not poor! We have got money. And if you cannot afford, then I can send my personal nanny in school to do these task. How dare you make my child participate in such activities!'" Listening to this, of course, I was too hurt with the kind of mindset the parent carried. Is it really so, that if you have got money, then you can make your child dependent on people to do some basic tasks in life? Are parents aware that if their children consume their language, thoughts and mindset, then these children will never be able to respect people and treat them as equals? Even if I keep aside the community and world, what would be the impact of such a mindset on a child's wellbeing and life skills? Will this child ever have the confidence to handle tough situations or be able to do basic tasks if the foundation was full of support and help? I mean, I am sure adults are aware that no one lives forever, then how are they sure that they are going to be around the child whenever he or she would need them? Pandemic has taught us to live independently and do our tasks on our own. If not, then what else will?

Well, what has happened, has happened however let us understand what would these activities do to the child's development. When children are involved in their daily routine task such as

1. It is dinner time, would you like to help me arrange the dishes for all of us on the table or floor? (however, the family or school prefers to set up for meal time)
2. I am going to bring dried clothes from the outside and fold them, I was wondering if you would want to join me?
3. Let us prepare for bed, let's get your blanket.

And various other activities, such as, arranging and sorting utensils after washing them, arranging shoes in the shoe rack, etc. all such basic and safe tasks that children can freely take on with you.

For example, while the child is sorting and stacking utensils he or she explores pre-math concepts of shape and size, number operations by counting. In fact, each task at home somehow lie within the wide area of the learning frame for pre-schoolers. Each task will give children an opportunity to recapitulate concepts and explore patterns, shapes, colors, materials and senses, and engage in counting, stacking, classifying, data analysis, problem-solving, speaking, learning names and letter sounds.

So, imagine you are contributing more towards learning than anything else. The first lesson we must reinforce is that learning is a continuous process, do not demean the process by dividing early years into study time and play time. There is no such thing as study time. Children learn even if you are not teaching as they have all the super powers that they need to learn and that varies from child to child. Each one has its own super power to learn. Whether they go to school or not, whether they have got thousands of books or not, learning is always in progress. Hence, our only job is to provide them with resources and experiences.

9. Gratefulness journal

They say, the sooner the better; I say, that's right! I do regret not learning things in my childhood and today they are just challenging to learn. My regret lists includes not learning how to skate, swim, and not taking active part in athletics. My head enjoys all three activities but my body just doesn't have any experience of it. And so the neuron is pruned for those activities. I am taking you to Jean Piaget's theory of cognitive development. The research lays emphasis on the significance of early childhood years i.e. 0-5 years as crucial learning years. I want to share one of my articles that talks about the rationale behind it.

Ever since I took child development seriously, I have believed that learning begins from the mother's womb. This concept is not new, this is right from our existence. Have we missed thinking on these lines? Do preschools uphold the same beliefs in terms of learning or do they only talk about so-called innovations?

When I was a child, I heard a story, however, the context of the story has witnessed an unpleasant revision in the recent past when I encountered parents going to parenting coaches or for counseling. The story goes like..."Once there lived a demon 'Hiranyakashyapu'. He was against God and wanted to take revenge in his lifetime and wanted people to consider him to be their God. His wife, Kayadhu, conceived a child when Devtas and demons were in conflict. Kayadhu was taken away by Indra, and Narad Ji interfered and made him realize that Indra was wrong in doing so. To save Kayadhu, Narad Ji took her along with him to his Ashram/gurukul where she was safe, away from the war. Kayadhu, throughout the time only heard the chanting of *shri hari, vedas* and the name of God. To the knowledge when Prahlad was born, the first thing he said was "*Jai shri hari*". And became a great devotee of Lord Vishnu."

Now then, what happened in the story? How did a demon's child become a devotee of God?

The answer to this is "Environment". The environment provided to the child right when he is in his mother's womb is of utmost importance as it helps in shaping in thoughts, ideas, emotions and connection in relation to the world. This is how we get to see the world. We fight, shout, speak lies, break rules, be untruthful in front of our children and demonstrate that they can also behave in the same way. The way we behave in front of our children has a major impact on how they perceive the world around them. For preschools, at the foundation age of the child, it is very important to focus on what they are making children see and how.

Now that I am following the early childhood... ah leave early childhood... following the Preschool Industry where there is an increase in the number of preschools. I feel this is an opportunity for us to have so many preschools but my question is "Is the existence of a preschool making any difference to the child?" "Is the model helping us to provide a foundation to the child to be able to grow as a global citizen?" It is not what we do, it is what we believe and are intentional about. Actions without intention will not give any outcome. Everyone is talking about education with emphasis on much content a child is consuming in a day. Do we think that there's a correlation between how much information we have and leading a contended life? We teach children today about four seasons, but do we really have four seasons in the months we mention in textbooks? The education system will not change just by talking about it, schools will have to implement and think mindfully about what they really want to contribute with this tool. From what we see today, the main objective of educational institutes is improving the literacy rate. Education is beyond having knowledge; it is about how we deal with situations in life, mindfulness, working on ourselves.

When children fight in school we try to solve it by telling them who did what and apologizing, sharing a consequence, etc. Why can't we help them resolve it, by providing them time to talk about how it happened and what can we do to actually resolve the thought and manage emotions rather than controlling and closing the matter for them.

For parents, teachers and preschools, it must be difficult but let us start being conscious about what we serve our children at home and in schools. The four important factors that we need look into are as follows:

1) Have dedicated conversations with children and encourage them to ask questions;

2) Get involved when they are playing, talk to them about what want to do next in the game;

3) Provide education and not literacy only; and

4) Do not panic about what they will miss or what isn't there. Focus on what is there and create immense opportunities to gather new experiences.

***"Value-based education is the present and future."*-** **Shruti Nagar Dave**

That's the power of foundational years that we have as a gift to contribute by nurturing a mindful human. So, this activity is mostly either recommended to be done first thing in the morning or the last thing for the day. Remember, young children learn by observing and imitating adults hence model this habit of writing a journal each day for the child. This activity is not just for the child, it is also a practice for adults that will transform and elevate the highest form of vibe of 'gratitude' in you, and you will radiate the same energy that will keep the environment positive.

Here is what you need for this activity:

1. Self-chosen journal or diary (for all members)
2. A dedicated area to do this activity (praying space or writing table or room, as per your preference; choose a space that makes you feel inspired)
3. Pen or marker

Once you are ready to begin, firstly thank God for the day and express gratitude by saying a prayer. I am truly happy to share with you the prayer that I say and it goes like:

I thank you, God, for today,

I am thankful to you for providing me

with all the necessary resources

you blessed me with food, water and air.

I thank you for protecting and blessing me

with all the experiences in life.

I am open and ready to radiate

love, peace and happiness in the world.

I mean you can create your own affirmations that you value the most and you feel grateful for. You might want to ask your child, "What is one thing from today that you'd like to thank god for?" Or, you can ask them to simply write or draw three things that they are happy about today. If the child is not yet at the writing stage, ask them to paint or paste relevant photos or pictures in their book. Make this a daily activity to explore the power of a positive and mindful lifestyle. For effective and instant results, ensure you continue and consciously model and demonstrate the behaviors and habits that you are willing to nurture in your child. It becomes confusing for a child when they see you fight with someone for something, and on the other hand, you tell them not to fight when the child is only imitating the action they observed in you. .

Have you noticed that recently adults under the age of 22-45 years are more inclined towards watching inspirational videos, listening to podcast on self-development, finding true purpose, listening and sharing affirmations and positive quotes on social media? The year 2020 witnessed a sudden wave that shifted the interest people from becoming a billionaire to leading a minimalistic life. What I am trying to convey here is 'the sooner the better'. In other words, when children wear a gratitude cap on their head all the time, with the help of such mindful practices, at home or school, they will be the future adults who are self-confident, high on self-love and self-esteem. How many of you just began to imagine your children living their life with the highest vibrational energy? At the same time, how many of you feel bad about having gone through such experiences early in your life that put you in a box of self-doubt, insecurity, anxiety, stress, and made you into a risk-averse person who is a people pleaser and is far away from living in present?

Reflection:

1. Create your own gratitude prayer. (What are you thankful for? What are you grateful for today?)

2. What are the five values you wish to imbibe to set an example for your children?

3. Which are the three habits you want to give up that are impacting your child?

4. From the above list of activities, which three activities will you implement at home or in your class?

5. If you have to define learning based on this chapter, how would you define it in two sentences?

Reader's journey so far

Take some notes and share your experience of reading the book so far. What are the things that surprised you? Mention if there are any questions that arose in your mind. Write down any challenges that you think you might encounter if you implement the learnings from the journey so far in real life. Write how will you overcome those challenges to provide the children high-quality foundational years.

CHAPTER – 5

IT IS NOT ABOUT LEARNING IN A SEQUENCE

I learn what I see first, I learn what I touch, I learn what I hear, I learn what I experience! Learning is in the present, learning is on the table and in the materials around me, learning is in the language of my friend and family, learning is in what I consume; learning is from the problem I solve, learning is in the failure I encounter in play, learning is in trying again, learning is by accomplishing a small task, learning is in play when I eat when I care and wash my feet.

– Shruti Nagar Dave

[Hi, can you provide the syllabus of the play group class? What will my children learn? By when my child will learn to count to100? How many letters will my child learn in a week and which form do you teach first, capital or small?] I have come across so many questions similar to these, and I say they are valid. In the age of fast communication, excess of information and access to the world in a click, worry and doubts pertaining to -whether or not have I put my child in the right school or am I providing him/her with better education, etc. are bound to arise. I totally empathize with parents. Imagine, you go to buy a toy, amongst thousands of stores online and shops you pick one place and from that one place where there are so many toys, you pick one for your child. Hey, let me give you a reality check, ready? Here is the thing, imagine you take your child along. Ha ha... I just heard many say, "let's not talk about that though".

Now, you got one toy finally home, and one of your friends asks you, "where did you buy this from?" You say you bought it from x place, and they reply, "oh, I heard there was an issue with the quality." And there you go. The best you got, is now a case of doubt and more over that is the guilt of putting so much effort yet not getting the right stuff. But is it something that has to do with your store choice or the influence that our friends, brands and commercials have on us? The same thing happens when it comes to choosing the right school for children or an educational approach. You do a lot of research and find that the active learning approach is most effective; you start implementing it by making your child focus on the process of learning, experimenting, working with materials, learning to read with help of the whole language approach. Your three years old can count till 10 and also have a one-to-one correspondence with numbers and objects, can also identify before and after numbers and another friend of yours says, “My child can rote count till 50, what about your child?” Think about what will you do? The first thing is we ignore how much our children can do and focus on what they can’t. This is the cause for this doubt which later impacts the child’s confidence. You just simply forgot that one more than 10 is 11 and so on. Your child is now aware of this pre-math concept. This is a skill, and not just a memory test of memorizing numbers till 50 and rote counting without any connection to mathematical concepts such as, what comes after, before, what is number two? Actually, it’s about looking at math as a real-life concept rather than printed numbers and formulas. We do math in our everyday life by asking how many *chapattis* do you want? How many windows do we have in our house? Can you bring me a pen? By having books and picture books that children access that has page numbers and numbers printed on it, drawing conclusion and estimating, which bowl has more food? Body parts and other concepts naturally encourage children to do the math.

I learn what I see first. I learn what I touch, I learn what I hear, I learn what I experience! Learning is in the present, learning is on the table and in the materials around me, learning is in the language of my friend and family, learning is in what I consume, Learning is from the problem I solve, learning is in the failure I encounter in play, learning is in trying again, learning is by accomplishing a small task, learning is in play, when I eat, when I care and wash my feet. Here is the preschool syllabus for those who keep looking for it. Each day at preschool children learns and explore the following. Each day! It is not today we will learn square shape! That is not how learning takes place.

To understand it in depth, I want you to walk with me into a visualization of a two years old child and experience how the development takes place.

Kripa is a two-year-old child. She is exploring toys with her playmate; she has got blocks, a sponge, paint brushes, loofah, wooden spoon, bangle, bowl, and some paper. While Kripa explores all those materials using her hands, mouth and feet, she experiences the textures and feels of the materials. The adult around Kripa notices and write the observation as well as providing vocabulary and labeling her experience with materials as below:

"The brush feels **soft** on your skin."

"I notice you **are creating sounds** when you hit a bowl with a wooden spoon."

"I wonder what will happen if we **dab** the sponge on a water plate, would you like to try?"

"The paper feels **light,** I see you are having fun **tearing** it."

"I notice you are hearing the tearing sound."

"Paper is **lighter** than a block."

"The wooden spoon is **bigger** than a paint brush."

"Bangle looks like a **circle**. Do you wish to **trace** it on the paper to draw a circle."

"How many blocks do you have? Would you help me count?.. one..two.. three.."

Adults' job here is to talk about the actions the child is taking without adding their own judgments and opinions.

Here, adults need to label what the child does and share their own experience. What happens when you do this? The child learned concepts namely material sounds, soft and hard, light and heavy, big and small, fine motor through tearing, observation and experimenting (when they explore sponge soaking water, blocks for counting. Now, it doesn't matter if the child does not verbalize the learning yet or recognize letters or numbers. Our job is to speak and say 'what it is'. Formal education takes care of the syllabus and formalizing learning as they are preparing for public examination in the future. I do know many schools that are progressive and unconventional and taking stands to work with children by focusing on the learning process. I recommend parents who really care for learning must explore schools that follow active learning, project-based, and inquiry-based learning approach. I mean let go of your anxiety and fear of missing out and be open to what is new for your children. Again, I'd like to reiterate, learning is anyway taking place. So in the preschool, the first session won't be let's learn letter A, A for apple, B for ball and singing without any connection or context. Good schools won't worry about teaching the letter A and then sequentially other letters. They know that each child is unique, and how children learn is an amalgamation of the development stage, child's interest and content as derived by HighScope. In preschool, the online sequence is to be consistent and explorative with the materials, people and experiences. All you need is to understand that the research foundation like HighScope has been built over the years and it has got standards that we must be aware of. Children in their early years already have a lot to take on, so they need to build connections and learn to play in groups, they work with adults and peers to break stranger anxiety and separation anxiety.

This reminds me, adults need education to look at children as an individual, because they look at them as a child, every problem they face or anxiety or fear they have is shattered and invalidated. For example, the child gets scared of your friend who visits you and starts to cry. You become embarrassed and intend to please your friend who must not get offended. So what do you do? Some of us might say, "She always does this! Uff! Why are you crying? See, he is your uncle, say hello!" Blah blah... Let's see how and what the child is feeling: "Dear mom and dad, maybe he or she is your friends but I do not trust him/her yet. I have no connection yet, they are stranger to me and I am uncomfortable when you force me to say hello.'

There is a lot that is caused by the unnecessary competition, me v/s you, better than them, and what did I miss. All of these thought bubbles make us get toxic ideas and we put children in a similar kind of environment and that is the damage done in the foundational years. It is important for us to discover what is competition and whether or not it is good for children. By the way, is it a right idea to strive to be a number one always? May I ask you, how do you define winning and losing to your child? What is it for you? While you reflect on it, I can share my thoughts on this. Given millions of children facing competition in schools and at home unknowingly, it is important to reflect upon its influence. We have been listening and saying things like, "Competition builds character and creates excellence". Everywhere you go, or watch television, all you see is competition everywhere. Our society has got carried away with the need to be number one. As adults, if you are in business, you say, "We need to be number one in x business"; if you are in a job, "You get ranked based on the targets you achieve and get acknowledged in front of colleagues for the sake of healthy competition". Be it at school or home, we have always been pushed too hard to become winners and the continued the assertion that competition can be healthy and fun if we keep it in perspective. It is not that the competition is misapplied or not understood. The problem lies in the competition itself. The phrase "healthy competition" is actually an oxymoron.

I have been all my life participating in competitions and got used to being first, second and third. So how has that influenced me? I certainly had become aggressive and the fear of "Cannot afford to fail or lose" took a toll on me. But is this healthy? No, not at all. With this kind of personal experience and after having studied the best research and debates, I am sharing an approach that you can work on with your children. This approach is known as cooperative games. Pause for a moment and reflect on the results you to want from this approach for your children. Possibilities are that you may want them to cultivate healthy self-esteem, to accept themselves as simple human beings. You want them to become successful, to achieve the brilliance of which they're capable. You want them to have loving and supportive relationships. And you want them to enjoy themselves. This is fine. However, it is important to bear in mind that competition isn't always necessary to achieve what you want, rather it's your commitment to the task and time that will help achieve your goals.

So, what does competition promote? Especially, when it is from early years...

1. Hostility

By definition, not everyone can win a competition. There is only one winner. This means that each child comes to regard others as obstacles to his or her own success. Above anything else, this is one primary thing children would learn through competition.

2. Aggression

In young children, where it is possible to learn empathy by the age of seven, having control over one's emotions, such as aggression isn't an easy task, especially when it comes to a competitive environment where it plays a crucial role. Children show aggression because they have difficulty dealing with their anxiety or frustration and can't verbalize their feelings as others do. The aggression may also be a form of impulsivity. So, if we are not sure as to how children will respond to competition, it can prove to be toxic.

3. Fear and resentment

There are agreeable benefits of competition, but the harm it does outweighs the benefits. So, what is the alternative to this?

Cooperation, on the other hand, helps children in communicating effectively, building trust in others and accepting those who are different from them. Why cooperative games in the early years?

1. Child is at a time beginning to see others as human beings;
2. Child is beginning to enjoy playing with others;
3. Child is yet developing empathy;
4. Child is at an important juncture in life for developing trust; and
5. It helps children develop a friendship with others.

Let's take the example of a traditional game that you have played in your childhood. Now, think and change it from a competitive to a cooperative perspective where no one loses and see what is possible. (Reference: Moya Fewson. She was my trainer and coach at HighScope preschool curriculum certification in Michigan, U.S.A).

Sports are all a different spirit, but only a perspective can ruin it or create it. Before going into the bigger idea, cooperative sports can be a now and future. Doing the thing right at "Now" situation will favor life, then sticking to the old methods in any given situation.

How can parents raise a cooperative child in a competitive world?

Comparison is very natural for human beings. You like something over others based on the comparison. It certainly cannot be nullified, however, there are affirmations and an environment we can provide to children. We can have a conversation that can be encouraging and promoting cooperative perspective in day to day life. In order to fit in the real world, competition is only life boat for survival.

Raising healthy, happy, productive children goes hand in hand with creating a progressive society. There are better ways for our children and for us to work, play and grow, acknowledging competition is all based on myth.

There is already enough conflict and hatred in this world to produce more for our future. It is time when the other side is nurtured with friendship, collaboration, oneness and teamwork.

There is never a problem with children, it is always our expectations that produce conflicts. The development of a child can be easily explained. Think of your child as currently standing at level one; now, all we need to do is to work and provide resources and experience for the child so that he or she can reach level two. Now, how do we know which level is the child at? Here you need to pick one of the approaches that have developmentally appropriate milestones. Also, what your two-year-old child can do will differ from other two years old. So, there mustn't be any comparison. All we need to focus on is to help children move developmentally from where they are to the next. The Reflection section, given at the end of this chapter, will help you understand and acknowledge your expectations as adults from the child and the reality. It will help in designing a bridge that will provide the child progressive experiences in the foundational phase.

In simple terms, the more the exposure, the greater the learning. Children have natural instinct and curiosity to explore and discover the world, all we got to do is provide them the resources and language to relate with it.

Reflection:

1. According to the age group you deal with in class or the age of your child, list down the expectations you have from the child in terms of learning and knowing.

2. What will you need to do to let go of your expectations?

3. List down things that your child does and that makes you feel proud.

4. Which incidence do you recall when you invalidated your child's emotions?

5. What change will you make in your approach to support the child to learn at its own pace?

CHAPTER – 6

IT IS NOT ABOUT LEARNING MANNERS AND ETIQUETTES

"Do not make learning forced or so significant that children begin to hate it. Trust the process of life. They are children not robots to behave the way we want."

– Shruti Nagar Dave

I just learned how the water roles from the table; I discovered that the paper cannot soak the water; I learned to run at a speed and you kept a glass full of water on the floor; I explored that ink and colors take time to fade away from my clothes and face; I just tasted the color and mud, it looked like food; But when I demonstrated my learnings to you, you shouted at me and said, "stop making a mess!! Where are your manners?"

The silence you just experienced after reading the above passage is exactly the purpose of it. The early years or say, preschool age, is for children to be open to possibilities of learning that are endless. Well, in this chapter we will explore how can adults introduce 'manners and etiquettes' in early years without making it a forced behavior. We will explore some cases where there is an impact of the language and word we use for children and the tone in which we speak to them.

What are manners? It is a conduct, or a way person behaves in a situation. We talk to children about stories or manipulate their thinking by saying, "you are a good girl" or, "you are a good boy", Why? Because the children fulfilled the expectations you had from them. I have heard this analogy from my spiritual guru in his lectures, let me share it and that surely will give a context about this chapter and where we are heading. (I have added a bit of drama to it).

One day a mother is speaking to a friend on phone and she asks her child to bring a glass of water for her. The child gets up and brings a glass of water for her mother. The mother proudly says, "See, I told my child to bring water for me and she got up at once. I must have imparted great values in her upbringing." After a while, the mother asks the child to bring a book from the table right next to her. The child is working with blocks and trying to build a tower and so is engaged in the activity. Her mother, again requests, "child, please bring my book that is next to you, you are mumma's good girl, right ?" And the child is not paying attention to it. To which the mother reacts, "I never taught you to disrespect elders. You do not obey at all, bad manners!" The child now looks up and tries to correlate what just happened with these hurtful words of the mother.

So, how did a child, who was labeled as a good child, the next second turns into a bad child? What were the criteria of both labels? Did the mother pause and think and observe that when she demanded a book, the child was busy doing something of his own and was fully focused and engaged?

Very early we tag children with phrases, such as, good, bad, disciplined, well-mannered and well-behaved. Some schools even give it in writing, "Kripa, is a sincere, well-behaved child". Here certainly well-behaved child meant, a child who obeyed all your rules, instructions and suppressed his or her expressions to avoid scolding and punishments. The same reports are shared with pride in the community as if it is an end title.

Many of us expect our children to learn manners and etiquette in preschool age. These include the following:

1. **Table manners:** It means that the child learns to not spill the food on clothes and table or floor. I remember listening to a complaint by a parent who said, "my child is holding the a fork in the wrong hand, why don't you teach them about it? Also, he forgets to wear an apron, this is what my child learns from the school?" Ahh! Ok, so how

many of us wear aprons while we go out for dinners or daily wear during meal times? By the way, let us first discuss what is an apron and why young children wear it? They are asked to wear it so that the clothes they are wearing are protected from the stain. So whose problem is that? Adults, as they will need to wash it or it will look dirty on the child. Hmmm, so the question is, do we spend time sharing this context with the child? Well, how will a child learn about the stain? In this scenario, I would have recommended parents to send a spare unused t-shirt and let the child eat and learn to eat independently with a spoon, not to forget in this age they are also exploring moving their small muscles. And when they spill, they experience that it got dirty and it is time to clean. When you clean the shirt, take the child along with you let the child see how water and washing powder help remove the stain. After few attempts and experiences, the children begin to become aware of the fact that they have spilled food and eventually learn to take care of the spill. We do acknowledge that while the child learns to eat the food independently, they are also exploring hand-eye coordination, gripping (small muscles), holding a spoon, distance and speed. Hence, do not worry much about spilling and spoiling clothes. I guess the freedom of learning and exploring at this age will set the foundation for children to discover their learning approach.

2. Discipline: The most dangerous word it is. All my life I had a different perception of discipline. What is discipline? Google says, *the practice of training people to obey rules or a code of behavior, using punishment to correct disobedience. Oxford dictionary:/ˈdɪsəplɪn/[uncountable] the practice of training people to obey rules and orders and punishing them if they do not; the controlled behavior or situation that is the result of this training. The school has a reputation for high* *standards of discipline. Strict discipline is imposed on army recruits.* I am sure we sense the threat that a child might get here. Imagine a bird that has not yet learned flying is asked to not hurt anyone on the flight, not to flap the wings on others, to stay in the nest when it is sunny, stormy, windy, cold and rainy. Ha haha, while I type this I imagined a baby bird who is thinking, *why don't you give me a chair and TV to watch forever. If flying has so many problems, what do I have wings for?*

The matter of the fact is that we give general instructions to children and our actions are sometimes opposite to the instructions we give. For example, respect elders as they are older to you, do not eat junk food it is not a good habit, and so on. Imagine, you tell your child to always speak the truth and never lie. Now, one day your neighbor is at your door and you instruct your child to lie that you are not at home. Your child tells the neighbour, "Aunty, my mother told me to tell you that she is not at home."Loads of laughter and embarrassment at one time! This is where children face conflict and experience the difference between what adults say and do.

Therefore, generalizing the concept of moral values and telling children about it is not going to help them understand and have an appropriate conduct as per situation and time. You don't need to tell the child to speak softly in the temple. Do you know why? Because the ambiance of the temple is set, so when a child sees that everyone around him or her is quiet, silent and praying, they know how they are supposed to behave in such a situation. For a moment, even if a child speaks loudly he or she acknowledges and corrects that. That is the power of demonstration and environments that gives children the experience of the appropriate behaviors. Now, when you take the child to the park he hears sounds, noise, fun, watches other children play and run, and there the child will do the same as the message reaches to them when they observe the surroundings.

Our focus hence is on providing them the experience of different situations and appropriate behaviors. Letting them have exposure to the consequence is effective than threatening them for punishment or bribing them with gifts to behave in a certain way. I made a short story to give a glimpse of the power the words hold in nurturing children in foundational years. It goes like, "A little ant was once told, 'Hey, you are as strong as a lion'. Since then she worked hard to be a lion. One day, her mother told her, 'You are an extraordinary ant'. And she gained her confidence back." Like this ant, we must not forget our roots, who and what we are as that would help you elevate to the appropriate next level. We misjudge our identity based on what people say and that's the real downfall. And this is what our children need to hear from us that they are who they are and they are loved and accepted for who they are.

Children will show up as likely what you believe of them.

Reflection:

1. Think of an incident in which you reacted to your child's behavior and tagged it as 'bad manners'. Mention it below.

2. In which place or when does your child express themselves like happy birds?

3. Can you think of an action or a situation in which you scolded your children and it developed fear in them?

4. What will you now say to the child when he or she makes a mistake? What will be your language like?

5. Convert the discouraging sentence into an encouraging sentence:

Discouraging:

"Stop making a mess, only bad children do that!" (Imagine your child spilled water on the floor)

Encouraging:

"____

____

____

___________________________."

CHAPTER – 7

IT IS NOT ABOUT GOOD HANDWRITING

If all children have unique hands, why are we expecting all the children to have 'good' handwriting. By the way, who came up with this idea of labeling handwriting as good or bad?

– Inquires the child whose handwriting was labeled as 'bad'

In the preschool age, children are getting familiar with the idea of expressing their thoughts and understanding with the medium of writing. They explore letters and letter sounds, picture books, print in the environment, observing different letters written differently. They are having first-hand experience in using writing tools. Having said that, I am going to inquire about why do we lay emphasis on good handwriting at this age? First of all, the children will begin to go through all the pre-writing stages such as grasping objects, holding things, using colors and paints, scribbling, making lines and spirals of different sizes, long and short strokes and eventually letter like forms are visible. But our expectations at a very early stage becomes of good handwriting.

It is because adults, while teaching children to write recognizable fonts, expect 'good handwriting' and so, the satisfaction of the writing level's accomplishment is never matched. Hence, children are asked to practice more by filling tracing books. And before even getting a proper connection with the letters, children are expected to write in cursive handwriting. Our ultimate goals should be to teach children write with legibility — as far as we can read it. When we talk about preparing children for the future, we somehow need to cover all the aspects. Children these days have access to screens and gadgets. Let's think about this, how many of us have observed our children typing messages or letters on WhatsApp? How many of them can send audio messages? Last year, there was a sudden transition for young children to the online classroom. They began to explore keyboard/phones earlier than our time.

So, children are moving in the direction that is designed for time, the path that will lead them to their careers and future.

Writing foundation is about children understanding that we write to express our thoughts and ideas. The HighScope education and research foundation has insightful research on developmental stages of writing. The emphasis of preschool age is on the foundation of writing i.e., pre-writing skills. In this stage, children explore their small muscles and experience grip. Working with play dough, sand tray, tearing and pasting activity, squishing toys and lacing activity and more.

Well, you could find many resources on pre-writing skills and various activities that help your children experience the same. But here I want to highlight the impact the comments such as, good or bad handwriting, has on children. First of all, handwriting does not define your character. Ah this takes me to an incident, told by my co-researcher. Once she went with her mother for a PTM and she got her work displayed. Her mother was a bit worried about the handwriting which was not as she desired. She said, "you lost a score because the teacher could not understand your handwriting". And her classmate heard her mom being upset and he intervened and said, "Aunty, look at my handwriting." Since then the girl became conscious of her own expression. We need to first acknowledge that there are various stages the child goes through before he or she begins to write. The foundation of writing is not about knowing how to write in good handwriting but practicing to work with the small muscles in play fine motor development, commonly known as pre-writing skills. Many adults provide children tracing sheets even before children are comfortable with paper and pen and other tools. Initial years are for children to experience and explore working with writing tools and some activities that build a foundation for writing commonly known as pre-writing skills. That could be opening and closing the bottle cap, holding and grasping objects with one hand, scribbling, play dough, sand tracing and so on.

Later, children work on connecting with the objects, sounds and words (labels). It is like children learn at an early age that writing is to express ideas however as adults, we are fixated on the idea of how clean and good the handwriting is. The difference here impacts the child in approaching writing as he or she moves to the next levels. Some children even start running away from writing. So, some progressive and active learning approaches suggest strategies to support children inculcate interest in writing. I recommend you to read more on this on HighScope's website or other credible sources. But my experience with children says that we need to learn about what they like and build activity around it instead of the 'have to' kind of environment.

Handwriting does not define your character. It is what it is. Who you are is beyond that or much beyond that. We need to be conscious of how and what we comment on children's work. Is it elevating the child to the next level or making him feel threatened? Our expectations from children in terms of their handwriting need to be realistic. If a child writes in readable fonts and with spacing and other writing schools, we have nothing to worry about. It is important to accept their handwriting as unique as they are. All we can do is to provide children with comfortable space to write and, writing tools; providing them the opportunity to write about topics they are interested in also encourages them to experience purposeful writing. One of the possible ways, as I have shared in previous chapters, is writing a gratitude journal or notes to express how they feel. They can even use initial letters, drawings and scribbling to convey what they want to. If you do not understand the message by reading or watching, simply ask children, "why don't you tell me more about what you have created?" instead of saying, "what is it, I did not understand". Invalidating children is a big no; acknowledging where they have reached and giving them a way to move to the next level is a big yes.

The point is to appreciate children for who they are. Adults must be conscious of their certain expectations. Those expectations come from either their own failure as a child, or fear of survival. Being relevant is the key, what is required right now for children is what we need to arrange, support and provide. Nothing else would matter if children explore things they can work on. We must set an example for the child to appreciate others for what they are good at by appreciating our friends and family. It takes years for someone to discover who they are. Well honestly, it takes births to get to that inspirational side. However, if I limit this conversation to the material world, then it is only about discovering what you are good at and what the things you need to learn, and what certain things you acknowledge do not serve you anymore.

Imagine a very young age child who says, "I thank God for all that I have and I am open to the new learnings that are planned by Him on my way to push me closer to the discovery of who am I." This is totally possible, but only for those children who are surrounded by adults who live this lifestyle. So, it is not about having good handwriting or being known as a disciplined child or a talented or intelligent child; what matters is our own learning, the path we chose and the wisdom we carry. Let me ask you, you were once asked as a child, "what would you want to be when you grow up?" Think of an answer that you gave a long time ago, and relate your life right now. Is it that? Or on the way, you are still discovering , who you want to be? It is because you are not the title that people give or the world defines you. You are a soul and until that is acknowledged by us, the arguments, debates and fights in the world are going to go long. I'd say, you think of world peace as an impossible concept looking at the current scenario then listen to this, if we adults, nurture children responsibly and mindfully by setting an example for them, by providing positive and affirmative space, we would we pretty close to that concept of peace. And because that is the limitation of humans, we are where we are.

Reflection

1. What were you told about your handwriting when you were young?

2. Do you see the impact of what was said to you when you were a child in your approach to learning in life? Has the comment impacted you in any way?

3. Have you commented on your child's handwriting directly to the child or spoken with teachers about it? How would you like to rectify that and turn it into a positive approach?

CHAPTER – 8

IT IS NOT ABOUT TRAINING TO BE IN A RACE

"Stop teaching children to prepare and work for job security. Teach them to be a free agent way early."

– Shruti Nagar Dave

The times are tough, yet promising, this is said by almost all the people from different generations. The first-hand experience of anything new is always full of anticipations and worry, and later we adapt the same as if we were born with it. My parents nurtured me to be unique and stand out from the crowd, always unique. And what it did to me is really special, it made me become comfortable with myself; if I am alone, I do not get depressed because I enjoy my company. I have the power to create the world the way I want in my head. Even while I am writing this book, I am thinking about why did I write and when I looked at the number of pages, I said, "that's really something". I do have a voice to share. I feel grateful to God for this blessing to celebrate life by trying new things, learning from them and moving on. My journey in the education industry with parents, teachers and children actually began from working with children on fields associated with NGOs. I closely worked with children on the ground, those children who came to school for half a day and the rest time they used to sell water pouches or helped parents at the roadside or selling things on the street. It was inspiring to see a child selling water near a Joggers Park in Ahmedabad. I recognized the child as I used to teach him in a government school as a volunteer from Samvedana in Ahmedabad. I learned early in life that the purpose of education was bigger than what it looked; it involves a lot of contribution than just running it schools as a business.

EdTech companies that received huge investment in 2020 and 2021 as promising ventures for future education, in my opinion, that's good for business however a big deep dent on the soul of education. I fully relate to parents when they say, they are confused as to who to trust. The influence of media is so high that you are shown visuals, advertisements and videos so much about a product or brand that your mind connects its familiarity and you end up buying it or being its consumer. You must be wondering why am I talking about business and advertisements here. Simple, today, schools have become a marketing-dependent service and product. Well, now I am confused about whether to put it under the category of a service or product.

Some schools have their development and marketing teams larger than the academic team. This can tell you about the prime focus of any preschool. Now, is it only about the preschool, schools, or brands? Nope. As people, we too are influenced by the trends around us. Who would you trust more – a brand that is promoted by celebrities or a small school that is run by a passionate early years expert who is not active on social media? Well, option one will be easy to explain to people where your child goes, the second one will have you create credibility in your social groups.

Not all of us walk that path. I am awestruck by some parents who want to go with what works for children, their trust in teachers and research. The problem here is not schools but the mindset. In my college times, the design of the race was that if you are pursuing BBA then the next step is to apply for CAT, SAT, ZAT and so many other entrance exams and the target was no less than IIM Ahmedabad for MBA. I mean that was the design. Only some of you might have quit the race to pursue a different pathway. How many of us actually dare to leave the race when we see millions walking in one direction? Who would take a U-turn? It is tough!

Preschool years play a crucial role in providing children the kind of exposure that would help them build connections with themselves, other people, materials, community and the world. This is not the time to count the number of things children do or say, but rather the focus should be the amount of exploration, inquiry and participation children make in day-to-day activities. Every child has his or her own set of experiences in life, interests and pace of learning. There was a time when there were these cute baby contests in Delhi NCR, I mean only when I moved to Delhi I discovered such things exist. So later, I discovered that those contests happened to get more attention from potential parents amongst them some parents would take admission. And parents began to get involved on Facebook by posting their baby's picture and asking their family members to like, comment and share. It was a literal act of crazy marketing stunt that led to a trend and there we go. Social media was never meant for children and now it looks crazy that the apps designed for adults have more feeds for children. Isn't it? Some claim that it boosts confidence in children and takes away their stage fear. What???? Ok so that confidence that they already have is shattered first by invalidating their anxieties and then making them face the camera to regain the trust. I did speak to few parents about what exactly are they doing by posting details, videos and funny distorted face videos on their social media? One of my friends said, "It is just like an activity, my child is interested in this." So I changed my question to who introduced social media to children and was it in natural interest of the child or it started as below:

"Come up, show Mumma how you make face when you are angry? Don't look at Mumma, look into the camera?"

Half of our life goes into seeking validation for what we can do from others and the other half goes into realizing that we must not seek validation from anyone. Like they say, the sooner, the better. At an early age, if we provide children with the kind of exploration where they experience that it is not about resources but our resourcefulness in life. It is not about how many toys we have, but what we do with them. Children already are in their own discovery in preschool-age right from what they like to their dislikes. At this age, they are in the stage to distinguish themselves from others and appreciate the diversity in the community. We, adults, have missed things in life in our clouded minds hence when it comes to children we wish that they get everything on time, rather before time. But what is bigger than time? Nothing. It is only our inconsistency with what we believe in that is highly influenced by what is going around. And as a result, our relationship with children and relationship with self gets complicated.

I want you to discover with me why do we sometimes end up getting influenced to join the race? What is it that we fear taking a risk and standing out in the crowd? I mean, not in all areas of life, however, each one of us does stand out in at least one area of life.

For starters, this has to do with our foundations, our values and the environment we lived in our early years. My husband and I were discussing the same when I put this thought on the table and we ended up sharing some childhood episodes that layered our personalities. I am going to take a very authentic episode we shared and got our own discovery. My husband always talks softly and he does not appreciate talking in loud or fully expressed tone, as he says we live in an apartment and it may disturb neighbors, like in flats and apartments are designed that way. On the other hand, I have a different approach, I said, "it's my house, I should do what I want." And that's how we ended up thinking what's the matter here. Upon sharing, we came across that my husband has lived in an apartment, closer to neighbors and he was shushed and stopped while he played cricket in the house, the people living on the floor below would come and ask him to reduce the noise or avoid playing cricket. And of course, parents would consider it. Now in this shushing, it added the layer for him that we must not be loud it is not appreciated or it reflects a lack of discipline. On the other hand, I have lived in a tenement in my childhood and I used to scream, shout and fully express myself in the house and outside. And I do not remember to be shushed, so for him, I lack discipline in this matter. So imagine our childhood experiences layered up us to be how we behave individually and the way we express our thoughts and feelings.

Now then, when we have discovered the impact of childhood in our life, I wrote this chapter to discuss how much it matters to a child to be heard, encouraged and have adults model certain behavior for them to learn from rather than just making comments or correcting them by saying, "hey that's not good manners", or "good girls don't shout", "good boys do not make noise" and what not.

So these minor, tiny and unconsidered experiences also build our personality, which is layered from the inside. Children are always fully expressed, high self-esteemed and curious. It is only when the adult's pre-set experience and judgments are showered upon them with comments and ideas which conflict with children's natural self and in that confusion, they do what they are expected to do eventually. I call it the suppressed version. That is why we get included in the race to avoid the shushing, and judgments or be called out of the group. However, an extraordinary individual is one who discovers the root of it and resolves the same. Children are already having all the color they need called life, however, some superpowers are victims of dents put by the adults they begin to trust. To have children be extraordinary and live life with experience and expression, it is vital for adults to model those super powers by letting go of their anxieties and fears and being conscious of what they share, demonstrate and tell to children. As I mentioned earlier, children are likely to be who you think they are. So even a single doubtful comment or casual judgment will mean something for the child's growth and development. Adults can begin to turn around the attitude here but accepting which places are they fearful in life, what are the things they regret that they did or could do? What major childhood experiences they have that they found to be the root cause? And later, clear the mind and look at the children as an individual. It's like an opportunity to provide environment and resources to your younger self, be it your own children or class children.

Adults can pick up the below practices, to begin with, and provide an open-minded space for children to grow:

1. Saying sorry and apologizing to children when it is your mistake. It is important to ensure that you state the mistake. So children know what are you apologizing for.
2. Asking children's consent before taking any decision or call you to make on their behalf.
3. Beginning to involve children in family decisions (of course, age-appropriate ones). For example, if you are buying a shoe rack, show them pictures and ask which one will look good in our house.

4. Acknowledging their choice before who forces a decision upon them. For example, you want to go to your friend's house and your child at the same time is engaged in an activity and he wants to complete it. Rather than saying do this later and invalidating their work and value for time and demanding the child to stop playing and come along. In these situations, we sometimes threaten them, by saying, "are you coming with us or we will lock you and go". No, No, No!!! You could definitely say, "I think you are working on something, can I know how much time will you take to complete it, I would really like you to join us to visit your uncle's house". Yes, yes, Yes!!! We need to really shift our mindset and consider how we speak to children.
5. Looking at children as an individual in place of looking at them as 'kids'.
6. Practicing to highlight the silver lining in the low situations.

Reflection:

1. Which practice would you implement from the five of the listed practices for providing open-minded space? And how?

2. Can you think of an incident where you thought you should have apologized to your child or children?

3. What is your discovery about the root cause of the layer on your personality that stops you from taking risks?

CHAPTER – 9

THE RIGHT ABCS OF PRESCHOOL

There is no right and wrong in anything, it is just the side you pick. You have full freedom to choose what works best for your children, but the condition is to understand their needs at the moment.

If you are reading this page, I cannot be more grateful to you for your time and trust in hearing my voice through this book. There are several books available by extra ordinary writers, education experts even excellent blogs out there, and for someone like me writing this book was important as I consider myself as a responsible education enthusiast who cares about the stakeholders and wants them to know the different sides in foundational years of children. This chapter talks about the right ABCs of preschool, as in what can we expect and look for in preschool-age for children.

1. It is teamwork of parents and teachers. It is in fact a team work between the research, parents, teachers and children. It surely takes a community to nurture a mindful young mind.
2. It is a transition from home to school because children connect with the outside world through their interactions and connections with things, people and the environment.
3. It is about learning through purposeful play.
4. It is about learning as per the pace and interest. The more exposure to the content, the more is the learning experience and development.
5. It is about making errors and learning by doing. It is about encouragement and acknowledging the attempt.
6. It is about writing to express one's ideas and thoughts. It is about exploring writing tools and becoming

comfortable with writing from bigger-sized letters to writing in a small space.

7. It is about letting children explore more, discover more and experience more. It is about observing them move from one interest to the other.

8. It is about the freedom to express and learn.

There is no right and wrong in anything, it is all our understanding. People do not see what you see even if you think they are seeing what you are seeing. There is this old-aged example of people defining an elephant by few blind folded people. I wonder, we adults experience conflicts like difference of opinion between two people, juggling with our trust on people, pleasing people or being true to oneself, and more, then why don't we prioritizes working with children on bringing an open-minded approach towards life? I am thankful to God for this opportunity to share a mindful approach in preschool years and how can we nurture mindful adults. I am excited to introduce this idea to you all and cannot wait to hear from you after you implement it. Below are the practices and toolkit that will support a family in nurturing children in a mindful space. I must say, it is not only about children or for children because adults play a very important role in establishing a mindful practice for children by practicing it themselves. This only would work if you put 100% faith in its results, even if there is a doubt or inconsistency it must be redone by acknowledging what was not in place last time that made you give it up. Here is an approach that I have designed for you based of the learnings from the wrong ABCs of preschool years:

The Mindful Foundation (TMF)

What does being mindful mean? It is a meditative technique to practice to live in the moment, in present and in now. It means to be aware of, conscious of and being sensible. It takes years for anyone to attain the experience of the meditative zone, and this amazes me as I wonder, what if being mindful was in the foundational years of life, how would the world be? Won't there be more collaboration than competition? More acceptance than differences? More of love than hatred? More productivity and less casualness? More humanity than war? I mean if the foundation is about thinking from different perceptions and being open-minded, how would the people relate to each other as a community and as an individual. Such wonderment encourages me to continue to work and contribute to this industry. I believe that if I succeed in imparting my knowledge to even one family, the others will ultimately become beneficiaries of the same in the times to come. The more we allow children to think and share, the more will be their power to be a decision-maker as well as problem-solver.

Have you ever noticed when you ask your child to give you a minute and you'll get back to them, they get back to you within the time you said even when it cannot read the clock? It is because they live in the moment. Children work on what they have, talk about what they see, and share what they think without any fear of the future or grievance from the past. Now look at us, we adults speak to people based on our past experiences and agenda of future. Imagine you are walking on the streets and listening to music. You looked at the road going towards the right and you thought to explore new ways today. You walked towards there and did not see anyone else, yet you got your miles and you returned home. You tell your friends about this new route and one of your friends shares that the road was risky for anyone to walk alone. Would you now be confident to go to the same route again? Well, the incident I shared here happened to me in San Jose, California. What happened to me then? Well, I fed my brain with the anticipated problem and that got my brain categorize as danger. So my mind and body experience anxiety and discomfort with similar thoughts so even when I am in India and we are in a car, I am afraid of trying new routes. How many of you can think of something similar that your past experience comes in the way of taking risk? Since we are talking about mindfulness, I would like to ask you one more question that is, how does that relate to spiritual experience? We live in this illusion of having control of the things in our life. Our 'know it all' attitude is what makes us arrogant and we end up being close-minded people. It is always inspiring when I see people who are content in their knowledge and are willing to listen to someone else's perspective without invalidating it. They know that the world is huge and a human brain cannot know it all. In my life, I am grateful to be blessed by God that I could discover that I am a soul and I am here to discover the purpose of life. When we are under the influence of *Maya*, our soul struggles to pull us out with bad experiences however the influence is so much that without the willingness to discover who we really are, one cannot get to this path. Leaving arrogance and being open to surrendering to God is the way. However, some of you who are reading this may feel, "That's crap! I am the one who decides what happens in my life. I have helped people from dying... I have donated to x and y and so on." What did you hear from above? The only 'I'. And that is nothing but the ignorance of our arrogance.

The only certain thing is birth and death, what we do in between time, creates our values. Well, this is all a spiritual context that I have shared in my first poetry book which is on my journey to discover soul urge as a spiritual seeker. It was important for me to share the above context because mindfulness is not only about some scientific concept to work with the brain and learning how it operates. Mindful living is about experiencing life as it is, and discovering what is! Hence without adults working on themselves on this, children will not be benefited from any of the learning.

It is easy to design a mindful approach for children in preschool hence I offer you the below program which you can implement in your schools, or at your home. I have designed this for children, right when they are in their mother's womb till they are eight years old. I have named this program **The Mindful Foundâtion for Meaningful Life.**

It is imperative to note that there is no inherent meaning in life rather it's the meaning you add or give to it. And that is to live in the moment and serve the living. This reminds me of an interesting factor of happiness guilt which is an integral part of this practice. When you hear about someone's demise, the sadness that you experience is directly related to the level of attachment you have had with the person or say the soul who just left the body. How would you react if you got to know that you won a lottery or you have a newborn? You would experience sorrow and happiness at the same time. Well in this situation we try to be mindful by acknowledging what is, however not invalidating the gift of happiness by God. We leave our bodies when it is time. The soul was never meant to be forever in the body. And at this moment we experience happiness to guilt. How can I be happy when my friend or relative is sad? Somewhere our arrogance of the matter that my actions will make her feel better or I have control to make her happy is in fact had nothing to do with how your friend who is in loss feeling. Each one of us has our own journey feeling guilty to be happy when others are sad is not helping either. I may not have mastered this, but I consider it to be my responsibility to share this with you so that you know we all are walking in our own path and all we need to do is to take our actions mindfully that's all.

I am projecting some environmental errors we provide our children and that makes their belief and approach as to how would they like to relate with others. In this toolkit, I have shared few cases where if we take actions mindfully we could provide children an open-minded space to receive the situations. You could choose to pick one of such practices and implement the same for 21 days without tracing the results. In this, the outcome of your work will be in the experience and not in a form of yes or no data. Hope you enjoy working on the below practices to provide your preschool-aged child or children or class with a mindful approach towards life learning.

1. Do not vent out on children the toxicity we bring from the outside.

"Do not let those who don't matter enter your home through your mind and snub your family who matters, by your words that are the result of your unnecessary toxic interaction with outsiders."- Shruti Nagar Dave

This was an extraordinary discovery I have had, and I also know the impact being both sides as a receiver as well as a person who vented out. Hypothetically, you are at work or working from home, frustrated with your staff or boss; you are on social media for hours, looking at a hundred thousand people through a search you don't even know. All going into the trap of seeking attention for likes, views and comments on people. I wish all could actually find a purpose in life or at least acknowledge what is not for you. So letting go of the things that do not serve you well is going to benefit you in the future. In some conversations because you felt jealous, envious, or thinking to keep up to your place and continuously dealing with insecurity. Just after which you saw your children playing and singing loudly by running here and there in the living room and having fun. Seeing them do so, you got angry and reacted to used toxicity or foul language as a means to vent out your frustration. What wrong did the child do? In this case the adults reacted to the frustration they had with outsiders which they may not have expressed to them but vented all on the diamond-like family members who do not deserve to be snubbed. Hence this is the very important cleaning we need in our home, schools and in our minds. Cleansing toxic behavior is what is required when you are dealing with your child, without being getting affected by your past. There could be a lot of excuses for this, but feeling self-pity (self-absorbed unhappiness over one's own troubles) and saying that no matter how much effort we make, it will not add value to nurturing children. If parents are responsible to bring a life in this world, then they should always have the courage to nurture a young mind with an attitude that encourages peace.

2. Do not gossip and talk ill about others in front of a child

We do not get this sometimes that no one is bad or good. People are people. It's just that we need to find people who share common values and thoughts. It is important that we don't speak ill about others in front of our children as this sort of action can make children misinterpret people based on good or bad, and disconnect with them and their kind. Even if you say something which may not go well down such thing in front of the child you could talk about it.

"Papa is angry with his friend because papa expected this from him, and when he did not fulfil I got angry, but I understand that the reason why he did so. Papa will apologize for judging him quickly."

Or something that neutralizes the heat with a passive, compassionate and mindful cleansing.

3. Switch off from world and be home

One of the critical actions here is to switch off from your work and outside world when you are home at least for one hour. When you are home or off work or set up a time that will be your own time, keep your phone on the shelf or away. Pick only if it rings (the phone call), and shut all the notifications. In my phone there is this zen mode, that keeps my phone off the apps and only calls are working. Now be mindful or be present to see and be. You need to be doing things all the time, it is good to listen to your child as newly as possible, see what he or she is sharing, ask about the day and share some of the insights from your day. Inquire to children about when did they feel happy and what made them excited for today, what was the one thing that they did not like and what would they want to do now. Play with them as a child and see how they express themselves fully in this space where they are one with you. Encourage them to appreciate what they have and always say, "I am thankful to god for ______". Let your child complete it by adding what they want to. Do not underestimate or limit what your child can learn or do. Sometimes we think this could be difficult for the child and we stop ourselves from giving them exposure. Children learn what they see and from what they do i.e. experience. So be resourceful when it comes to interacting and offering children learning opportunities.

Set up your daily rituals as a family and meditate with the help of videos and audio available online.

4. Teaching children with an open mind

How many of us till today say, 'Sun rises in the east?'But the Sun is where it is, earth is moving right? How many of us teach children, 'Cow gives us milk?'Forages, we have been taught this and none of us questioned or corrected it. Even in schools or academic books, you will still find these sentences I am writing. How about the cow gives us milk? Really, does it? Or do we take milk from it? Sheep gives us wool. Really? Does it? Or we take its fur to make wool or should I say we take its cover to cover ourselves in cold. I know there are so many such actions that you may have thought of just similar to that. Now, not blaming or invalidating any thoughts or beliefs here but how about teaching children what it is? Like we can say that we take milk from the cow. Let us be thankful of that as a gift. They are full of service. When we say cow gives milk, like really how? Does she come to our doors? Ha haha, just imagine that! But this is where the mindful approach in early years reflects upon how we present the world to children in early years.

One classic example is the picture representation of ugly and beautiful, fat and thin as opposite words. In children's books, we see images of people who are labeled as ugly and fat. So what are you teaching children? Did you recall the image of a dark-skinned woman? Why no one yet questioned that and it is in a children's book. What surprises me is that these books still exist and can be seen in the hands of a minimum of one child in the billion. In addition to this, how about books in which the teacher is always a female and the doctor is a male? What are we teaching our children through these images? To just give a hint of the damage here, they look up to things the way they are presented to them. In a family where male members dominate females, children grow up associating weakness with females and power with males and vice versa..

This is where we need to be mindful of what are children consuming in the early years, as the future is in making. We must rather be mindful to talk about acceptance of the fact that each one is a unique being. Each one has its own strength and areas of improvement. Conflict ideas and beliefs are bound to exist in a society, but we must respect everyone, as what people do is a reflection of the set of experiences they have had. How would you do this? By sharing interesting stories that talk about community oneness, individualized approach, watching and knowing about different festivals and why they are celebrated. It is important to receive new information or get exposed to opposing thoughts and yet being neutral in response. We need to be understanding to others than to only expect others to understand us. This can only happen if we first accept and learn where we are in this and eventually draw the path to the next level.

5. Designing your mindful daily rituals

Every family or school will have its own set of routines and activities planned. Mindful foundation cannot happen by adding one session around it or once a week working on something. It requires a lifestyle shift to be able to live mindfully. There could be simple activities you could include in your day for children to experience mindful living. As I said, children are already much mindful than adults are as they are not cluttered or layered with fear of the future and baggage from the past. They spend most of their time living in the present time. For children, major learning takes place by what they see adults do and say. The adults whom they trust. For example, children enjoy imitating their mother, father, grandma, or any close guardian and teacher because these people are the people who are most involved with children in their foundational years. So what and how they learn, they use words or language used by adults, they dress up or use a prop that makes them look like them. Sometimes children like to their father's shirt or mother's scarf. Children also sound like teachers or parents or adults at home. In today's time, when children are exposed to a lot of information when they access WhatsApp even if they cannot read, or when they play with blocks and the television set is on and some soap operas going on. When adults talk and speak about things, children do get access through listening.

Hence sit as a family and design your own plan that includes mindful activities, such as gardening, cooking, meditation, filling up gratitude journal, participating with adults at home in daily chores, organizing toys and belongings. This is to support children in being independent thinkers.

All of it will shift the way we think and look at learning in children's life. When we acknowledge that the learning never stops and it is a continuous process, our thoughts and actions will be relevant to our children. . One of the other things I would like to voice out is gender sensitization. I remember interacting with a boy while he was playing with other children. I was observing children playing with various tools and materials. I walked into the class and inquired what were children up to by asking about their work. While I was doing that, I heard a boy saying to a girl, "You are a girl, play in the kitchen". Listening to this I was a little stunned and had a big question on my face. I sat next to the boy and asked him, Me: Hey (name), I was thinking to ask if you could say more about this, why do you think she should work in the kitchen area?!

Boy: She is a girl.

Me: Yes, she is a girl, but even boys work in the kitchen, right?

Boy: I am playing with tools, that's for boys...

I settled the conversation by listing examples of various male chefs and female engineers. However, this anecdote impacted me to my core, and I wanted to discuss the same with his parents. After I gathered the information, I realized that the child was merely imitating his father and grandfather. I requested parents to break the ice on the subject and worked with them to give a new learning experience to the child. Later, the boy began to role play as a chef and became comfortable playing with mixed-gender groups. However what I discovered here is not just about what children get from the home, but also from our very own television commercials and advertisements, cartoons and soap operas.

See if have heard the comments mentioned below in general:

√ Colors: Pink is for girls and blue is for boys

- √ Cartoon/superhero: The protagonist is always a boy (Nobita, Noddy, Chota Bheem)
- √ Boys should play with cars and girls with dolls
- √ Video games are for boys
- √ Cooking is for girls
- √ Boys don't cry, they are strong
- √ Why are you crying like a girl?
- √ Girls are emotional and weak
- √ Girls should sit properly and not laugh loudly
- √ Girls should have fair mark-free skin.
- √ Classical dance is for girls only
- √ Playing table is for boys
- √ Family business is well run by boys, girls cannot understand business.
- √ Girls do not opt for mechanical engineering
- √ Boys do not opt for B.Ed. or home science
- √ Ladies don't drive well

(Reference: Research paper by Miti Nagar on Gender sensitization for B.ED)

Why should boys have all the fun? Well, now that certainly is a question I never ask. We need to get something here, what we think or say directly or sarcastically impacts the child. Half of the problems in the world exist because of the misunderstood mindset and context of feminism and gender equality. Nowhere it says it is all about girls or boys, we need to educate ourselves to speak as we mean and as we want others to speak. If you are angry and upset with some situations and your comment or post on your social media or debate with people, we must first look at what are we teaching our own children. A few people get enlightened to work on improving themselves. Whatever role we play, there is always a scope of improvement in it. The life is for us to identify who we are and discover the soul's purpose. To escape from getting known for who you follow spiritually, religiously and in life, we bring in logic, science and finding out where has it been proven as research. To avoid receiving questions and judgments; to be accepted as a part of a group with common thoughts, we say, this is what I heard or read, I am not saying it. This is a sign of self-doubt, lack of awareness of who you are and being open-minded.

Children must be given the opportunity to get feedback on their work:

When we keep praising children for their every small effort, it makes children settle at minimum level without striving to learn more or do better. However, if you are not around, and since they do not receive appreciation or praise it will have a major impact on them. In a world where we are judged on what we say and do, it takes a lot on a doers part to keep up. Before we even talk to children about it, adults must reflect on this themselves:

1. How do you feel when someone criticizes you?
2. What is your reaction?
3. Do you give up on it or lose confidence?

Now hear me out, how many of us thank people who once gave us feedback and showed us where we lacked? I remember I used to feel so bad when anyone used to point out my gaps because the entire childhood of my generation was only in two parts 'good' or 'bad'. So either you can be good in something or bad, there was no way of consideration of the learning levels or a midway. Either you are intelligent or you are dumb, there's no middle way. And this was only in the language of the community. When I was in 7th grade, I remember hearing my relatives talking about me to my mother or other people that the other girls are smart and intelligent they always score 80% above in exams. And I was a child who scored less than 80%. No matter what talent and intelligence I had as a child, the judgment of my relatives was so imprinted on my head that I began to rebel. Today, we are fortunate enough to have access to research and books all around the world that pave way for a progressive and positive approach towards learning. Hence it would not be fair for us to repeat the same mistakes that we had in our early years. We need to teach our children to become collaborators and not competitors, and leaders, not rulers.

Most people relate the quality of life with what they do or what they can afford but the quality is related to how rich you are in practicing to be humble, mindful, spiritual and open to life. In all, our children need to connect more with who they are than being a people-pleaser. And how can we do that? By setting up an example for them by demonstrating and acting on what we say and modeling out the behaviour, we can expect from them.

The expectations we have from preschool come from our regret of the past and fear of the future. Can you relate to the points mentioned below?

1. What I missed as a child?
2. Future is competitive, my child must know everything
3. My child must be perfect in all that is taught

4. My child needs to get personal attention
5. Money can buy anything and so is the learning experience
6. I want to put my child in the best school or online school to show I can afford
7. My friend's child speaks fluent English at the age of four, preschools must teach my three-year-old to speak fluent English
8. I have taught my child everything at home, like what is this? Child says fan and so on. Now preschool must put my child to a level up and teach more.

And the list goes on...

It is not a problem to ask for the best for your child, but the problem is when the best is based on comparison with other children. The right ABCs of preschool in one line could be – a transition from home to school, where children will explore the world and their connections with materials, people and themselves. I am a staunch advocate of active learning that is based on Jean Piaget's cognitive theory. Adults must read more about how the brain development takes place and similar work to stay on with this thought and provide children the environment they need to have a strong foundation.

Meanwhile, preschools must consider the essence of early years with the view of children. We do need more schools for sure, more teachers for sure, however those schools and teachers who do not enter this industry do some business or find an easy solution to start something of their own. People who run schools, preschools and even their own private coaching have a huge responsibility to nurture children in a positive, research-based environment.

In place of launching private personalized educational theories that are claimed to be a unique philosophy, getting along as a community as educating people on the source of the philosophy would really reduce the confusion, educate people and have more clarity on what can be expected in foundational years.

At last, I want to say, you cannot 'right' what you are not willing to confront. People mostly hide in the 'fit in' so that they do not have to confront themselves and discover who they really are. Hence keep looking for what do we need to work on as adults and being open in approaching children. Be it a school or a teacher or guardians or an education enthusiast, we all need to be involved in continuous learning, upgrading and self-realization to provide young minds with mindful living.

Summary

It indeed is a tough task for parents and teachers to be on a watch for what information and experiences children are consuming, however, it is certainly the responsibility of adults to provide the best of the resources and mindful environment in the foundational years of a child's growth. It is a choice to take responsibility as adults and contribute to a larger picture. Our focus is on survival for children, as we have for ourselves, and based on that we anticipate the future. However, the magic is in looking at the possibilities of life by appreciating what children are doing and learning in their own way and at their own pace. In a week, you can have a day to notice how many times in a day we end up comparing our children with others or ourselves. "When I was your age, I used to do..." this and that. but is that helping anyone? Even when you have a toddler, you need to be conscious that what you are thinking is being communicated to the child through your energy. The speaking is just evidential. Hence, I wanted to gift this book to you to support you in your journey with children. This book is your reflection diary, whenever you wish to let go, recreate, touch base on connecting with mindful practices for you and your children or your class. I would say research is still on, as we say each child is unique, each one is different, we must also acknowledge that even the observation or the way young children work will require constant observation and participation. And this is going to be forever. The needs and requirements of each age group, each child is different, hence keep exploring, sharing and inquiring to have best for children.

AFFIRMATIONS

Here is what people who trusted the approach and words have to say about their experience with the Author:

Sakshi Trehan, Curriculum Designer and Educator- "Teachers are the lights of our life. They sculpt us to bring the best out of us. They are the people whom we respect and admire the most. I met her for the first time during my teacher's training phase and I wanted to be like her. It felt I had found my idol. She is one of the most hardworking, creative, and knowledgeable people I have ever met in my life. I was lucky enough that I got a chance to work under her guidance. She is not only my manager but she also plays a very important role in my life. Her approach towards life is so amazing and spiritual. Her positivity enlightens my path. As an educationist, she fully supports every teacher and staff by encouraging them to continually learn, develop, and, perhaps most importantly, become leaders themselves."

Harleen Kaur, Educator- "I first met her three years ago. She is a unique, gifted listener and always open to help. I have never known another person who is so much in tune with herself and others. She is a great guide. I can truly see her ability to help people to find themselves. Recently, I was going through a tough time. I talked with her about how I was feeling and after her messages, I felt lighter. I am now a different person and have begun to see things in a different light altogether, and it has helped in moving forward in life. I have no words to express my gratitude to her. Thank you so much Shruti ma'am for being there for me. Looking forward to more spiritual guidance from you!"

If I Were a Child I Would...

(Complete the sentence given above)

Write About an Incident from Your Childhood Days That You Would Want to Undo. In the End, Mention Two Things You Learned from It and You Are Grateful For.

My Mindful Practices

What I Gave Up	New Habits

Our Family's Mindful Gratitude Prayer

As a family, let your child drive this activity and together create your own gratitude prayer. If you are an educator, create a prayer with your class children.

www.ingramcontent.com/pod-product-compliance
Lightning Source LLC
LaVergne TN
LVHW042351150826
845671LV00002B/85

* 9 7 9 8 8 9 4 1 5 9 0 7 2 *